Duncan:

May you be at peace & happy
in your new life. Peaceful Blessings.


Debbie:

Sorry for the loss of your
precious pet. Wishing you
comfort and healing.

Belinda

# Dedication

I wish to dedicate this first book to my parents.
Without them I would not be here, and I am
so grateful for their love and support.

I also want to thank my feng shui teachers, who
have taught me so much about the fascinating
art of Feng Shui. I feel blessed to be able to
practice and share this art with others...

Professor Lin Yun, Ron Chin, Nancy Santo
Pietro, Jon Sandifer, Howard Choy, Raymond
Lo, Denise Linn, and Elliot Tanzer.

and with special gratitude to Professor Wang
Yu-De, my master teacher in China in Classical
Feng Shui. He truly embodied good feng
shui with his kindness and generosity.

Thank you to my favorite authors who have motivated
me over the years to stay on my highest spiritual path....

Louise Hay, Marianne Williamson, Deepok Chopra,
Wayne Dyer, Shakti Gawain, Miguel Ruiz, Carolyn
Meiss, Iyanla Vanzant, Eckhart Tolle, Joseph Campbell,
David Hawkins, Ram Dass, Esther and Jerry Hicks,
Gary Zukov, the Dalai Lama, and Thich Nhat Hanh.

To Oprah Winfrey and Cesar Milan for
their great work and inspiration.

And, of course...

my dear little Yorkie, Bellaluna, for the joy and laughter
she brought to my life. She left this world too soon.

# Feng Shui
## for the Loss
## of a Pet

Restoring Balance during Grief and Loss: A Personal Journey

Belinda G. Mendoza

BALBOA
PRESS
A DIVISION OF HAY HOUSE

Balboa Press books may be ordered through booksellers or by contacting:

Balboa Press
A Division of Hay House
1663 Liberty Drive
Bloomington, IN 47403
www.balboapress.com
1-(877) 407-4847

Because of the dynamic nature of the Internet, any web addresses or
links contained in this book may have changed since publication and
may no longer be valid. The views expressed in this work are solely those
of the author and do not necessarily reflect the views of the publisher,
and the publisher hereby disclaims any responsibility for them.

The author of this book does not dispense medical advice or prescribe the use
of any technique as a form of treatment for physical, emotional, or medical
problems without the advice of a physician, either directly or indirectly. The
intent of the author is only to offer information of a general nature to help
you in your quest for emotional and spiritual well-being. In the event you use
any of the information in this book for yourself, which is your constitutional
right, the author and the publisher assume no responsibility for your actions.

Any people depicted in stock imagery provided by Thinkstock are models,
and such images are being used for illustrative purposes only.
Certain stock imagery © Thinkstock.

Printed in the United States of America

ISBN: 978-1-4525-6683-2 (sc)
ISBN: 978-1-4525-6684-9 (e)

Balboa Press rev. date: 3/4/2013

# Table of Contents

# Introduction

This book is for anyone who has recently lost a pet or loved one, or whose pet might be in transition. I wrote it for my own healing, but it is my hope that you will find peace and comfort in reading it. I know that, when my loss happened, I wanted so badly to read something that would ease the pain.

I had imagined having this book finished long before now. It began as a journaling tool to help me handle the sadness I was feeling after I lost my precious Yorkie Bellaluna (meaning "beautiful moon") four years ago. I guess I needed more healing, experience and information before finishing it. So many people who have lost pets or loved ones have come into my life since my Bella died; I have helped many, and many have helped me. In this process, I have learned that timing is everything and things need not be rushed.

Today I am writing from my home on a beautiful but hot, sunny day in June in Austin, Texas. It is too hot to walk the dogs. I feel so sorry for pets out with their owners who are jogging in our hot temperatures. Owners have rubber-soled shoes, shirts and hats to protect from the heat. Dogs have only their fur, and the cement radiates heat. You can see them panting on their walks. When I can, I often stop and say something. At least carry water with you when running, to periodically give your dog some hydration. I am thinking of Bella today.

When my event first happened, being at home without my little pup was so difficult. I began writing down my emotions to help me through the grief. I needed to vent, to express, to feel. I didn't know how I would ever get over the pain of the experience; it was one of the worst feelings I had ever had.

After a few months I was able to heal some, and even adopted two precious new pups. At the time of the accident I could not imagine this happening at all. I had been so sad and in such pain that my whole body hurt, and I wondered if I would ever recover. As a pretty grounded person by nature, it took me by surprise how devastated I was at the time. Practicing the philosophy of feng shui helped me to overcome it. Its principles of being in the flow and not resisting things were at the core of my healing.

"What does Feng Shui have to do with grief?" you might ask. "I thought it was about decorating." While it's true that feng shui is known as the art of harmonious placement and is often applied to design, décor and architecture, it is also a healing art. That healing element is what drew me to this profession in the first place.

It has always been important to me that my work helps to transform lives, and feng shui has allowed me to do just that. The two Chinese characters Feng and Shui mean Wind and Water, two elements in nature that flow. Water you can see, but not wind; still, we need both. This is the yin and yang of life. Feng shui is about being in harmony with nature and also with yourself.

Grief and sadness are common, natural human emotions during difficult times, but restoring some balance after any painful experience is essential to living a happy life. Staying sad and lost in grief is not moving with the flow of life, and failing to get past those emotions can keep us stagnant and blocked. This, in turn, can lead to illnesses both physical and mental.

My own experience with the loss of something very dear to me brought me to this awareness, and after finding my own way past the pain and grief, I would like to share it with you.

You will find this book to be about much more than just the grief that occurs after the loss of a pet. My intention is to help you cope with the grief you feel after the loss of anything that was so close to your heart. This is the story of my journey and how feng shui helped me through it all.

Here is how my story began.

# The Shock

I am in shock. Yesterday afternoon I lost the love of my life, my precious Yorkie, Bella. It happened so suddenly, it feels like a bad dream.

It's 2:30 am now. I've been awakened by her memory and my deep, painful grief. I'm still shaking and feel nauseous. How could she have been with me just hours ago and now be gone forever? I cannot process this. I feel numb. I have never felt like this before.

We had a normal day. According to Chinese Astrology, it was a day of Good Fortune. Bella had been in heat; I was protective of her, as she was not yet spayed. She was 8 months old. I had planned to spay her a few weeks ago but the vet said he needed to wait until she was out of heat to avoid bleeding at surgery.

This would be her second time under anesthesia. When she was just 12 weeks old, she'd broken her little front leg and worn a cast for four weeks. Small dogs are delicate and susceptible to things like this. I felt really guilty about that incident, but Bella was fearless and independent. You couldn't even tell she was injured; she ran around with her little pink cast like it was her sword. Once the cast was off she was back to her happy, bouncy self.

Yesterday was a cool, lovely February day in Austin, Texas. Spring and fall here are just beautiful with moderate temperatures and low humidity. The rest of the year is another story, so I cherish our cool, brisk days.

I felt so refreshed as I prepared for the Chinese New Year. It is good luck to share a meal on that day to herald new and prosperous beginnings, and each year I look forward to inviting friends and clients to join me in celebrating. To prepare, I went to Austin's new Chinatown shopping center and bought some colorful Chinese firecrackers to place on my front door and ward off any negative energy that might affect the New Year. I also bought some fresh mums and orchids to adorn the house for good luck. They are not always available, but during the New Year they are plentiful and inexpensive at Chinese markets. In feng shui, the bright yellow mums signify prosperity, and pink orchids symbolize love.

While I shopped, Bella waited patiently in the car. She would rather wait there than be left at home. She was an "only child," and being self-employed I had the luxury of taking her everywhere with me. She was only 5 pounds, so I could often take her into stores with me in a carrying bag/purse. When taking her with me wasn't an option I would say, "I'll be right back," and after a quick look at me she would settle back into either taking a nap or watching passersby. I know dogs do not understand what our words mean, but it is uncanny how they understand what YOU mean when you say it.

I once had a black lab who would meet me at the door on her hind legs, bracing herself on me with her front paws. I would say, "that's not necessary", and she would get down. At 60 pounds, it was like a human giving me a hug. With her black coat, she was intimidating enough to serve as a deterrent to robbers but she would have just licked them to death.

My previous sales and marketing job had required me to travel extensively, and I hate to see pets crated or left in small spaces all day alone while their owners are working… so having a dog was not possible. I'd longed for a pet for years, and when I could finally have one, I was thrilled. I had chosen a small dog so it could travel with me easily.

On this day, when I returned to the car I put Bella on her leash and we wandered around the perimeter of the mall at Chinatown, getting a little exercise for both of us and leaving her free to do "her business." This was a familiar routine whenever she traveled with me on errands or to see clients. I had her dressed in a pretty pink and black polka-dotted sun dress with a pink bow and her pink collar.

I love the color pink, even though I don't wear it much myself, and it suited Bella well. She wore a pendant on her collar that was a peace sign surrounded by pink Swarovski crystals. She sparkled. I loved to dress her up to show her off, and she seemed to enjoy all the attention she received for looking so cute. Her tag was heart-shaped, with my last name and phone number on it. I'd read that it was a bad idea to put the dog's name on the collar; it might respond to its name if ever stolen... but Bella was so friendly, I don't think it would have mattered. I had taken her with me everywhere since she was a puppy, and that had made her open to everyone.

For eight months, Bella had been my constant companion – my friend, my little girl and my playmate. I'd never realized before how much I needed something like her to express my love. Being single, and leading a solitary life like I do, I've had some lonely times. I have chosen solitude to help me be at peace, gain inspiration, and be in connection with my higher self; I seem to need that to create.

While we need money to survive in this world, I have learned that abundance is not just about money – it is also about well-being. Money is just energy that helps us live out our passions. I chose to leave a hectic job that wasn't fulfilling anymore, so I could have more balance and peace of mind in my life. That search for tranquility was why I chose feng shui consulting as a profession. Bella was just one more thing that added joy in my life, something that had been lacking for me for many years.

I had been hurt by past relationships and I'd never experienced loving and being loved unconditionally before Bella. My relationships always seemed to center around conditions – not compromises. With Bella, there were no conditions. If I scolded her for something, soon after she would sit on my lap and lick my hands or feet, as if to say, "I still love you mommy, don't be mad at me." Now, I know pets are not people, but when you don't have children they become part of your family. And that's what happened with Bella. She brought love and laughter to my home, and allowed me to open my heart. What a gift!

# The Fateful Afternoon

fter we finished our walk around the mall, I decided to stop for another errand.

I had recently been informed that the house I was renting was going to be sold. I had just moved to Austin after 17 years in Memphis, Tennessee, settled in, unpacked all of my things, and made it "our home." When my landlord told me the news. I was just starting my feng shui practice again, and as a nester I'd been glad to put down some roots. Now I would have to uproot again... so my housing situation was weighing heavily on my mind.

There was a particular coffee shop where I would often take Bella on nice days. She loved sitting outside at one of the bistro tables with me, watching passersby while I read a book with my tea or did some journaling. It was a nice way for me to relax and wait for traffic to die down before heading home. On this particular day, there was a lot of traffic in the area and few parking spaces were available. My plan was to get my tea and go back to the car for Bella, so we could sit outside.

But today, the energy was different. As I was looking for a place to park, I realized that all the tables outside were taken. After another drive around the block I saw a table open up, so I packed Bella in her carrying bag and grabbed it. A group of about five men sat at a round table near the front door, smoking and speaking a foreign language I didn't recognize. I put Bella and her bag on a chair and asked the youngest of the men to watch her while I stepped inside for my tea; he said he would be happy to. In hindsight, it was risky. I had never trusted Bella to a stranger before, but for some reason that day I felt trusting.

I was gone for about ten minutes, plenty of time for something bad to happen, but it didn't. Somehow I had a feeling that she would be fine, and she was. When I came out she was on her hind legs, peeking out of her bag at me. I thanked the men, and they smiled.

On this cool and brisk afternoon, I sat in the sun and read a new book from one of the participants in the movie *The Secret*, about manifesting what you want in life. I had just heard the author speak at a seminar here in Austin and needed some positive reinforcement in my uncertain life. Would I have to move? Could I afford to buy the house I was renting? If not, where would I go? I had already been going through some turmoil over the past week regarding my career before I found out that my housing situation was up in the air as well. What a scary start to the new year! Lots of changes I had not expected. Ultimately I know change is good, but this was like the Tower card in the Tarot Deck: Upheaval!

I often use divination tools like ancient cards to help me connect with the messages my higher self is giving me. I'm a visual person, and the images on the cards reveal things to me quickly. Sometimes we are blocked and cannot see our way clear on things. If I have a question I'll wait a few minutes for the answer, then open a book; the first word or sentence I see often triggers something that is either the answer or a guide to the answer. This is me, accessing my higher power. This is how the cards work. In my practice, I use cards with beautiful feng shui images to help others with challenging life issues.

This day I was feeling overwhelmed. I wanted some answers and a way to feel better. Being outside with Bella, enjoying my herbal chai tea and reading my little book, was just the thing I needed before going home to face my troubles.

In retrospect, many things did not feel right that afternoon. As a feng shui practitioner, I do not like to sit with my back to the door; it puts you in a less commanding position. A solid back gives you support and a clear view of things, but I ignored the principle. I'm also allergic to smoke, and the men sitting near me were smoking… another concession I made to take the only open seat in the café that day. I could have decided to go home or for a walk instead, but I decided to stay

While sitting at our table, I put Bella down to stretch her legs. She seemed uncomfortable and wanted to be on my lap, so I pet her and massaged her neck and ears while reading my book. She was happy, just sitting with me and watching the people pass by. She always liked being at my viewpoint; being so little, she usually had to look up for everything.

Then the tragic chain of events started to unfold. First, my cell phone rang. I should not have answered it since my goal was to unwind, but I did. It was a woman who needed to talk about something painful that had happened in her life. We had met a week before at a seminar given by the man whose book I was reading. We had been e-mailing and talking about networking opportunities ever since. Bella was sleepy, so I put her in her bag while I talked. To make her more comfortable, I took off her leash. I would regret that decision later.

I would regret a lot of decisions later. Bella had looked tired in the car before we got to the café, but I'd chosen to go anyway. My whole purpose in going for tea had been to relax, but I chose to answer an unidentified call, instead of just letting it go to voice mail. My caller asked if I had a minute and though I was trying to relax, I said yes.

Unlike dogs I'd had before, Bella would just let me go on and on with people, never disturbing me. If we were at home, she would just go off and take a nap or play with her toys. Whenever I would get off the phone, I would often hug her, take her out, or do something else to reward her for being such a good dog. On this day, she stayed fast asleep in her bag while I continued with my conversation.

Another call came in while I was on the phone. It was a networking contact I didn't know, and I told her I would call her back. Taking the call was out of character for me; I rarely answer calls when I'm already on the line, especially when I don't recognize the number. But I guess I was so frazzled that day that I just wasn't thinking clearly.

I've asked myself over and over: How were either of these calls helping me feel better about my own situation? One of the reasons I went to the coffee shop was to relax, but these calls took me away from that. Walking Bella, meditating (which Bella enjoyed, often falling asleep next to me in the calm silence), or just going home were all better options than what I was doing.

I guess I thought talking to someone else would help me get my mind off my own problems. Distractions keep us from feeling our feelings. In my work, I help others solve their life issues. It has been a central theme in my life, and has sometimes been an escape from my own

issues. I often tend to the needs of others before my own...
something I have worked on for years. As the eldest child
and the only girl in a Hispanic family, I was raised to be
overly responsible -- but not always to myself.

# The Frantic Search

While I was on the phone, a large FedEx truck pulled up to the front door of the coffee shop. The driver slammed the back doors of his huge truck repeatedly. I could see Bella jumping with anticipation, fear, nervousness. I reached over to console her while still talking on the phone.

The next thing I heard was a very loud SLAM, which must have terrified Bella. She bolted out of her bag and onto the table, jumped over the chairs, and ran down the walkway like the speed of light. Instead of running down the store-lined pathways she ran across the street, where traffic was at an all-time high. I jumped up and told the gal I was talking to, "I have to go, my dog has run away." I hung up abruptly, threw my phone into my purse and headed off to find Bella. The man at the other table who had watched her earlier jumped up, too, and ran across the street after her. If this had been an average neighborhood, she could have run past fifteen houses in a row in a matter of just one minute. I often likened her run to that of a jack rabbit.

While Bella was not a Teacup Yorkie, she was still little. Her body was long, so when she ran she really looked like a rabbit chasing prey. Looking across the street, neither of us could see her. We knew she had crossed the street, but with all the businesses, restaurants, apartments, and parks in the area, where could she be? And how could we possibly find her? The man was across the street while I was still at the coffee shop. I yelled to him that I would get my car and drive over to make the search faster. He thought he had seen her go into a parking lot.

I frantically grabbed my things, got into my SUV, and drove across the street. The man helping me yelled that he couldn't see her any longer and went back to his friends. With traffic noise, we had to yell to hear each other. I began driving into the lot with all the high end stores and saw a well-to-do woman coming out of Talbot's, a woman's clothing store. I asked her if she had seen a puppy with a little pink dress running around anywhere. She said no, but offered to help me look. She took my number and then went on her own search in her beautiful Porsche SUV, leaving my number with the security guard of the shopping area. I drove further up the street with my windows open, yelling, "Bella! Bella! Bella!" I stopped everyone I saw and told them my puppy was running loose. A couple of people took my number.

I began to panic and cry, asking my guardian angels to help me find her. I pray to my Archangels for guidance, inspiration, and help; they are always there for me. My hope was that Bellita ("little Bella," my Spanish nickname for her) would go to someone and they would call me. Fearful thoughts ran through my mind, and I began to imagine her being stolen and never returned to me.

I felt an enormous sadness come over me as I drove without finding her. If she was lost, she couldn't last long without food and water. She could be attacked by a larger dog. She was so tiny. She would be so scared, too. I began crying more loudly. I asked everyone I saw walking: if they saw her, if they would call me? All were nice to oblige. One runner stopped, touched my arm through my car window, and said, "I feel your pain."

The lady driving around for me called to update me that she had not seen anything. Another call came in, which I hoped was a good sign. It was the woman who had tried to call me before, about networking. I was angry and abruptly said I could not talk because my pet was lost. By her response, she seemed not to believe me. I politely said I would have to get back to her. I was answering all calls at this time, in the hope that it was someone who had found my little Bella. Later, I was angry at myself for being so polite and apologizing to someone I didn't even know, when she was interrupting my search. Time was precious. I was in pain and it was okay to express it.

# The Dreaded Call

About 30 minutes into the search, the dreaded call came in. It was a veterinarian, who said someone had brought in a Yorkie with a pink dress. It felt like my heart stopped. I was so thankful. I said, "Yes, I have been looking all over for her." The vet said that one of her clients had found Bella and brought her in. She had been hit by a car when this man stopped and picked her up. By the time he reached the vet's office, she had already passed away from internal injuries. I found out later that, from the time she was hit to the time she arrived at the vet, only about ten minutes had passed.

In disbelief, I asked the vet if she was sure it was my Yorkie. The vet said she was wearing a polka dot dress and had a pink bow in her hair. "Oh my God!" I cried. I began bawling. The tears overwhelmed me; I could not hold them back. How could it be that I was just on a simple outing with my precious pet, and only minutes later she was dead? It seemed impossible. I asked the vet if I could see her. She gave me directions to her office.

I took the directions but of course could not find the place, as I was so distraught. I didn't really hear correctly. I called the vet's office number but could not get an answer. It was a recording. I was so frustrated.

I stopped at another vet's office in the area and asked them if they knew where it might be. I was crying the whole time. I felt like throwing up. I am surprised I didn't get into an accident, with the way I was driving.

I finally found the office, which was only five minutes from where I had stopped to ask for directions. I parked in the first spot near the door, which was for the disabled. I don't like doing that, but there were no other spaces and at the time, I felt like I was disabled. When I walked in, there was silence from the staff. They put me in a room that felt cold and sterile, with only a metal table. I have been in vets' offices before that were a bit warmer than this one. They needed some feng shui!

The vet brought my little Bella in, wrapped in a towel. Her pink dress, bow, and collar were all intact. She looked like she was sleeping but her eyes were open. There was no Chi. I knew in that moment that her soul had passed on. I asked the vet for a few minutes alone. I broke down.

I cried over her like I've never cried over anyone, saying over and over, "Mommy is so sorry, Bellita. Mommy didn't mean to be on the phone, Mommy is so sorry." I beat myself up for not being mindful. I was reading a book, drinking tea, talking on the phone, and not really watching out for Bella. I meditate on Sundays with a Zen Buddhist /mindfulness group; we always discuss ways to be more in the moment, focused, and mindful of things, people, and experiences. Today, I felt I failed miserably.

So many times when Bella and I were out together, I was not mindful. She only had her leash on about 50% of the time. With her in my bag, I had a false sense of protection. If she saw a squirrel she would dash off, and it took a lot to catch her. At 5 pounds she was fast, and she loved chasing squirrels. Yorkies are chasers. The breed used to chase rodents out of castles in Yorkshire, England; that is how they got their name.

In the vet's office, I prayed over Bella and did Reiki energy work for her smooth passing. Reiki is an ancient Japanese art of energy healing, for those who might not be familiar with it. As a teacher and practitioner, I use Reiki on myself for mind, body, and spirit healing. I had used Reiki on Bella once, when she broke her leg. She had healed fast and was playing and jumping around in record time. She would lie down and fall asleep every time I put my hands on her heart or chest or back. The warmth of the Chi flowing through her body healed her.

Looking back, I am surprised I didn't do more energy work on Bella that day, to try and revive her. Not that I believe you can do that, but what if the doctor was wrong and she was just passed out? It could happen. I guess I just knew. I saw no life, no breath, no gleam in her eyes.

I am also surprised I didn't stay longer. I guess I just needed to get out of there so I could really cry. The shock of it all had me shaking. It might have been helpful to have had a friend there with me, but it was late in the day and even if I could have reached someone, it would have taken at least an hour for them to get there. I guess I needed my own time with her.

The vet came in and asked if I wanted Bella's ashes. I wasn't sure, as I had not been through anything like this, so I said yes. I figured I would rather have the option after I was calmer. I wish now that I had asked for a lock of her hair, but I was too emotional at the time to think of those things. I hear this happens when people make funeral arrangements for their loved ones; making decisions in an altered state of grief is difficult. That is why it is important to have someone with you.

Still shaky and teary-eyed, I had to fill out paperwork at the front desk in front of the staff and pay $200.00 for Bella's ashes. It all seemed so business-like. What if I hadn't had the money right then? While the vet was warm and compassionate, her staff acted immature and cold. Why can't veterinary staff be taught some type of bedside manner? I had worked in hospitals as a medical social worker after college, and found many doctors and residents to be the same way. I wondered why they didn't teach compassion in their training. All the vet staff members had to say was that they were very sorry for my loss. When I paid the money, they didn't even say thank you, they just stared at me. At a moment like this you are feeling so vulnerable and fragile, any kind gesture of caring is needed and important. If I had received that kind of caring, I would have felt like returning and telling friends about that vet's business, but instead I have not been back.

When I left the office, I sat in my car and called a close friend. I left messages for a couple of others. I needed to talk with someone but just couldn't call my family yet. A good friend offered to come over, but I felt I just needed to be alone. Hearing someone else's voice was helpful.

# Coming Home

I drove home alone and crying, with Bella's treats in the front seat and her toys in the back. When I opened the door to my house I saw all her pictures and things, and that's when it really hit me hard. I had not experienced a loss like this before. People who do not have pets may have trouble understanding this, but they are not your pets, they are your family. Since I have no children of my own, Bella was like my baby daughter. She allowed me to nurture her, care for her, and be her mom. She definitely brought out my playful, spontaneous, and loving side.

I had Bella for eight wonderful months. She was with me 24/7. She led a full life. She loved people. As a baby, she went everywhere with me and people always wanted to pet her. On the way over to the coffee shop that day, she would rather sit on my lap in the car and look out my window than sit in her car seat. For safety reasons, I did this rarely. She would look over at me and lick my hand or my face, to let me know she was happy. She did not always want to run all my errands with me and would sometimes get tired, but she wanted to be with me more than anything.

On the day of the accident, Bella had low energy. I did not know this at the time, but female dogs can get a form of PMS, feeling lethargic much like women do. I should have gone home instead of to the coffee shop, but at the time I just wanted to take a break from my perceived problems. I say "perceived" because I do believe we create much of our reality. The depth of pain a problem causes you is due to your perception you have of the situation.

In Buddhism, it is said that life is suffering. This is called the first noble truth in Buddha's philosophy of life. It is our job to transcend the suffering with our minds. To say that life is suffering is not meant to be negative, but rather to help us see things as they are and then move into a happier place in our minds. I have come to like the phrase (and use it often), "It is what it is." When we change the inner, the outer changes.

I was trying to feel good that day. Sometimes if you can't change the feeling, change the environment and the feeling will change. This was my intention. Bella and I both liked being outside in good weather. She always garnered attention because she was so affectionate. If you came toward us and she was in her bag, she would get up on her hind legs and wag her tail to greet you. I had no idea this would be her last time.

I have had no sleep. I began writing this hours after Bella's death, at 2:30 am. Now it is 4:30 pm, 24 hours since her passing. The house feels empty.

Bella actually died at 4:05 pm CST, on the 5ᵗʰ day of February. In classical feng shui, five is not a good number. We were also in what is called Mercury Retrograde, where the planets are all backed up and the planet Mercury rules communication. It is a time of accidents. The chaotic energy in the cosmos can cause problems, like having trouble finding a place to park or sit, not being able to reach the vet when I called, and the Fed Ex truck slamming its door like it did. Regardless, I still took it out on the driver of the truck. I was so angry at him I couldn't see straight.

I am writing about this a whole day later and my head still hurts. My good friend Sara came over last night. Sara is a massage therapist and a very spiritual lady. She did some chanting and prayers over me while I lay on the floor, and then massaged my head and neck. It helped to console and relax me. This act was one of the most compassionate things anyone could have done for me right then... Sara just knew what to do. She also brought me a lovely card and a fresh rose, which I put next to Bella's picture. I thought I needed to be alone but what I really needed was a hug, and for someone to listen.

While Sara's hands were on my head, I had a rush of memories of my time with Bella. We had many wonderful and fun times in her short life. She met my friends and family, and everyone who met her loved her "spunkiness." I felt a rush of energy through my body when my friend worked on me and it calmed me.

It is important to reach out to friends at a time like this, even if it is just to talk about your feelings. If someone can be there and just listen, that person is a true angel. Sara did not try to comfort me with words, advice, or lots of talking. She knew it was a fragile time. The moments right after a loss are the most tender. I just wanted her there for her presence, to listen, and to provide a safe place for me to cry without feeling judged. That was her true gift to me.

Sara has now passed, at too young an age. It was unexpected by those of us who knew her. Vibrant, healthy, and happy, her life ended much too early. May she rest in peace, knowing she was such a comfort to so many, including me.

# Healing Tears

Tears are not a sign of weakness, but of strength. Many people are uncomfortable letting others cry in front of them when they are grieving. It upsets them because it brings up their own feelings of unresolved grief. But crying is needed to release the feelings, the sadness. The Universe is such a beautiful and perfect working system; I cannot believe it is a mistake that our bodies are made up of mostly water. When we cry we release the unneeded; we cleanse. There is plenty left over, so we should not be afraid to cry. Even if you are grieving in the moment for a recent loss, the tears can also clear out any past hurts and losses that might have been stuffed away.

I remember a time where tears were not considered appropriate. I obtained a degree in Social Work when I graduated from college, and my first full-time professional paying job was as a medical social worker. I worked for an international children's hospital, as a caseworker supporting Spanish-speaking families with children who were terminally ill. It was primarily a cancer hospital. Being present, listening, and supporting the families through whatever they were experiencing at the time was what I did. My listening helped to ease some of the anguish these families felt, seeing their children hooked up to tubes and needles and not knowing if they would get better. Later, after their children had passed away, I did my best to help them through the transition.

Sadly, most of the sweet children on my caseload passed away. Their ages varied, from infants to 6-year-olds. Sometimes when I walked down the halls to see my patients I would find worried mothers hanging out at the doors waiting for me. I couldn't always see them because I could only handle so many. At the time, I had about 200 families on my caseload, and I was just a young social worker recently out of college.

It surprised me that, after a child was pronounced dead, the nursing staff would immediately take the body to the morgue without giving the family even five minutes to mourn or say goodbye. It was a matter of fact, a detail that needed to be attended to as soon as possible so they could clear the room for the next patient. This act cut me to the core. As a medical social worker and advocate for the families at this hospital, I had clout. I would ask the nurses to return later, sometimes hours later, so the family had time to be alone with their precious children. I also asked the medical residents not to tell the parents their child had passed without contacting me first. If I was not around, they were instructed to tell the parents that their child had passed -- not "expired," which was the term they most often used. They are little human beings, not food items.

The moment of a death, whether expected or unexpected, is an intensely emotional, intimate, and powerful time, and it must be treated sacredly. If you cannot nurture someone experiencing grief, keep to yourself until you are ready to do so. No one taught me this, I just somehow felt it.

One incident I remember clearly: A little boy had a rare disease and eventually passed away. His family was indigent and the child was given what the hospital called a "pauper's burial." Within minutes of the child's death, doctors wanted the parents to authorize an autopsy for further research. The family was distraught at the thought of their child further poked and prodded, and they asked for my help.

I told the doctor that they would not allow it. As their interpreter, I relayed their wishes without trying to talk them into an autopsy, like the hospital would have wanted me to do. The child's body was put in a pine box with no padding of any sort and hauled off to a burial site, with the distraught family trying to follow behind in their car in the pouring rain. When they arrived at the burial site, it was raining hard. Dirt was poured onto the box and the hospital van left. This is not a way to die. We should die in peace.

The family didn't even know where they were when they called me. I gave them directions to get back to the hospital so I could meet with them for some final counseling. My role ended when the child passed in the hospital, but I had built relationships with these families and I felt the need to do what I could at the time. This was a reputable research hospital and many of the children had unique illnesses that were of keen interest to the medical staff. Once a child passed, the staff moved on to the next case as if the child was a lab experiment. While they did many wonderful things at the hospital, and although research is needed to save the lives of future children, the ones currently being treated need compassion and caring.

One thing that touched me deeply was how the kids would always have smiles on their faces, no matter how sick or bad they felt, knowing that they would be given some painful treatments. They lived in the moment.

When a child passed away, sympathy for the family would go a long way. The lack of empathy was one of the reasons why I left the field of medical social work.

I mention this story to demonstrate how important it is to be around people who can understand your pain and allow your tears when you are grieving.

# Rituals

I practice and use two types of feng shui with my clients. One is the Classical/Traditional Method, which comes from China and uses a Luopan (Chinese compass); the other, called Black Hat Sect, is popular in the U.S. I am trained in both and use an integrative approach that combines the two when helping clients. Black Hat offers spiritual remedies and cures for problems. I see myself as a healer of spaces more than a re-designer or decorator, although I love doing that part of my work.

One cure in the Black Hat Sect tradition involves setting up an altar to create a sacred feeling and lift the Chi (energy) in the space. In feng shui, incorporating the five elements in nature into your home helps create a stronger connection to nature or the divine, bringing a more balanced feel to both the space and you. The five elements are: fire, water, wood, metal, and earth. I love helping people set these up in their homes.

Altars are simple to create. Just add the five elements. Fire can be a candle; wood can be a flower or plant; metal, a bell or wind chime; water can be a bowl of water; earth, a rock or crystals. You can then personalize it by adding anything else you like... pictures of your beloved pet, items of theirs, etc. Place the altar anywhere in the home, except bedrooms or bathrooms.

Here is photo of a sample altar you can create and place on a table anywhere in your home. It can be as simple as this or as elaborate as you like. It is for your healing. The red candle is for fire, the bowl of water for the water, the metal incense holder for metal, the crystal for earth, the plant for wood. Fresh flowers work well. Place a picture of your furry loved one and anything personal of theirs.. Beautiful sympathy cards from loved ones who care can make you feel not so alone. The furry bear in the picture is the last thing I bought for Bella and the little dress it has on as well. You can move your altar around, keep it up as long as you need. It is not meant to be a death shrine but a lovely remembrance piece after the first few months of a loss. I found it helped me feel close to Bella and that later on I did not need it. Today, I only have a few of my favorite pictures of her up in my home. I don't need to be reminded of her death. I now feel her presence in my home and heart.

The first day of a loss is so painful. This was how I handled the altar ceremony at that time. One of the first things I did when I got home from the vet's office was to collect all of Bella's stuffed toys and blankets and wash them. It felt right. It was a cleansing process for me. (This is different for everyone.) Once they were clean, I put them in her crate. I felt compelled to set up an altar for her right away. Maybe I was hoping she would come back to visit, even if it was just for a moment. I took one of her pictures and put it on my dining table with the beautiful fresh flowers I'd bought at the Chinese market that day (orchids and lucky bamboo). I put her little dress, pink bow, and collar with crystal pendant next to it, along with some of her toys. In the end, I created a beautiful altar to see when I entered the house.

The flowers represented the wood element. I also had a candle for fire, Bella's picture in a pewter frame for metal, her crystal pendant for earth, and a bowl of fresh water for water. In this case water represented cleansing, but in Black Hat Sect feng shui it is also often used to absorb the stagnant energy from a space. If you go on a trip, for example, keeping a bowl of water on your altar will help to purify your space while you're gone.

A feng shui master teaches that pouring water into a cup three times with your left (or less dominant) hand and placing it on your altar daily keeps your space clear and sacred. The number three is a highly spiritual number, like the threes in the Trinity or body, mind, and spirit. Using the less dominant hand helps you let go of ego and allow the universe to take care of the details. I have done this for years. When I traveled a lot for work, I would come home and need to change the water because it had become thick and filmy. The water had done its job of absorbing any unneeded energy. I love that!

Since Bella never liked her crate, I did not crate train her; I used wee pads instead. I had read that Yorkies are hard to potty train, but I did not have this problem with Bella. She wanted to please, so she learned quickly. I kept her crate, just in case I ever did need to take her somewhere that it was necessary. I read once that, if you put a dog's food inside the crate and leave the door open, it will learn to see the crate as a pleasurable experience. The night she died, I refilled Bella's water bowl and left it outside the crate. I spoke to her out loud, saying, "Here's water for you anytime you want it; you don't need to go into the crate for it." It was the same water that I'd used to complete my altar area.

If I was listening to someone else tell this I would probably think they had lost their mind. Grief has you doing strange things. But there is some relief in doing rituals. They help you nurture yourself and commemorate your loved one. I have also read that the soul doesn't always leave quickly, so maybe Bella could see and hear me. I did feel her presence in the house on the day she died.

I have beautiful pictures of Bella, in nice frames, everywhere in my home. I had taken her for a professional photography session a couple of months earlier. I had a picture made of the two of us together; all the others were of her in different poses. The photographer really captured her inner joy and beauty. I loved dressing her up and showing her off. She enjoyed it, too. Her energy is all over my house. If I ever move from this house, I will take her memories with me. I kept her toys and clothes for a while, then donated most of them to a dog group and the Humane Society. I kept a few special mementos.

At the time, I could not envision ever wanting to go back to that coffee shop again, even though it used to be one of my favorites. In time I have been back. I remember reading that Jackie O never went back to Dallas after the death of President Kennedy. I can now understand why. It can bring up painful memories all over again.

When you lose someone after a long-term illness or due to old age, it is sad as you mourn -- but you have time to prepare for it. When it happens unexpectedly, like in a tragic accident, it is hard to believe. The shock factor is so strong that it lingers in your body, leaving you numb for a while. Do whatever it takes to feel better. Rituals help.

# Space Clearing

While space clearing is not a part of the feng shui art form, it compliments the practice wonderfully. Those not familiar with the concept might think it is "woo woo" stuff, but everything is made up of energy, and that includes thoughts and actions. Imagine moving into a home you just bought from someone who was ill or died while living there. You want to move in with your new furniture for a fresh look, so you clean the house really well. You get rid of all the dirt so it feels great when you move in. Space clearing is the same thing, done energetically. The idea is that energy in thoughts (such as the emotions involved in depression, illness, bankruptcy, divorce, etc.) can get stuck in walls. Then you move in and wonder why your relationships never make it, or your health never improves.

Native Americans believed in banishing negative energies by using sage, a dried herb. Many shamans and feng shui masters have developed other techniques to rid spaces of these energies. It is amazing how different a space feels after a space clearing. As a medical social worker (and even as a patient once in a hospital), I could see a need for space clearers. Each time a patient passed away in a room, someone else was placed in the same room later that day or the next. Of course they changed the sheets and cleaned the room, but all the heavy energy was left behind, like sadness, grief, anger, and fear.

There are many ways to clear the energy of a space, from smudging with sage (waving the smoke around the space and into corners of rooms) to prayers, energy work, healing oils, incense, drumming, and chanting. When I scheduled my hysterectomy I asked one of my spiritual friends to space clear my hospital room while I was in surgery, so when I came out I would come into a cleared room. It was lovely. My time there went well and so did my recovery. There are books on the subject and professionals to help with this process. I recommend it to all my clients and friends. It is an integral part of my work and is what I feel makes my feng shui consultations so successful.

After a month, I did a clearing on my home. Not to remove Bella's memories, but to cleanse and make way for new beginnings. It helped me to let go of sad feelings, feelings of loss, blame, guilt, etc. Space clearing resets your clock and places you in the present moment. You feel fresh again.

# Loving Speech

It is the Chinese New Year and two days since Bella's passing. I had already planned a dinner for some friends and clients. I really wanted to cancel it because I was so sad, but a good friend reminded me that I am always telling people what you do on the day of the Chinese New Year sets the tone or energy for the year. She said, "If you want to spend the year in sadness and grief, it's your choice, but why not celebrate Bella's life?" At first, I was upset at how insensitive she was. She did not have pets so I knew she couldn't understand. But then I realized that was my grief talking. Her advice was good. Darn, I hate it when people use your own advice back at you!

So I continued with my original plan. And I would dedicate the dinner to Bella, as difficult as it might be.

I held my head up and told only a few people at the dinner about Bella, so I could get through it. I gave one friend two large bags of Bella's treats and grooming things for her own dogs. She asked, "Are you sure? It's so soon." I replied, "Yes. I won't need them."

One of my friends at the dinner had some comforting words to say. He knew I was feeling guilty about Bella's death, and he told me there was nothing at all I could have done differently. "It was her time to go," he said. "Her time here was short, but look at all the joy she brought you. She wasn't meant to be with you any longer than this." I felt comforted by this, even though I still wanted more time with her.

Feng shui is about energy and harmony, and words play a part in that process. Words have energy. It is good feng shui to be compassionate, caring, and sensitive to others who are in pain. If you are not sure what to say, say very little and just be there for the person. Your presence is enough. My Zen Master teacher Thich Nhat Hahn has a phrase he uses often, which I love. "Darling, I am here for you," or, "Darling, I know you are suffering and I am here for you." Using loving speech can transform pain into healing. Don't worry if the person doesn't return your calls or doesn't want to talk right away , just stay in touch periodically letting them know you are there for them. When they are ready and need you, they will call or will let you know their needs. I heard a friend say that people will show up at the time of the death and be just wonderful with all kinds of support, but when time passes and you would love some company and to share memories, many of those people are no where to be found. Continue to reach out, it will be appreciated but do remember...

When people are in shock and grieving, it is the most delicate time. You feel like you would cry at a simple touch of your skin. Words said at that time are so important. If you are with someone suffering a loss, use words that are calming, compassionate, caring, loving, and concerned. This is not the time to give advice! Don't use this time to offer your opinion on what it might all mean. If a grieving person wants to know, he or she will ask. Above all, do not tell someone to get over it! Everyone has their time.

What I needed was for someone to pray for/with me, ask if there is anything that I need, call or e-mail to see how I am doing, or simply listen. Just knowing that people care is enough to help me get through. When I feel strong enough, I call the ones who make me feel safe to share. Those who are uncomfortable with death or who are just too busy to check in with me, I let go.

Each of my loved ones has responded in the best way they know how. This is not a judgment, just an observation. Some prefer e-mail, cards, no response, response through others, etc. I don't need a fleet of people trying to make me feel better. The right people show up when I need them and I know who I can call if I need to reach out. Reaching out is important.

# Good Deeds

In feng shui it is said that to live a good life, three things are necessary: good deeds, good feng shui, and destiny. We can control our deeds and feng shui, but destiny is the one part we cannot control. It is also known as our soul's purpose.

Destiny is why some people win the lottery, despite not playing the game very much. Research has shown that many lottery winners lose their millions, sometimes even after just a couple of years. If they squander it, are greedy with it, or use it just to accumulate more things, that is not good feng shui. I remember reading, "If it is your deepest intention to do good with the abundance that comes to you, you are more likely to receive it." If, for you, winning the lottery is about giving back, doing good for the community, having a socially responsible business, etc., then the chances of money flowing to you in that way are greater.

If we see everything in life as coming from Source or the Universe and Source is abundant and good, it makes sense. Money is energy, a vehicle for creating good in the world with a Buddha-like or Christ-like mind. Why wouldn't Source want to put abundance into the hands of someone who can make positive things happen in the world? This is one of the first principles of attracting wealth. See it doing as much good for others as for yourself.

The same day I lost my dear Bella, I called the vet's office and asked if I could have the name of the nice man who found her. If it had not been for his kindness, I would never have known what happened to her or been able to see her. Closure would have been impossible for me. I would always wonder if someone had stolen her. I would not have believed she was dead and might still be looking for her today.

So I called my Good Samaritan. His name was Jimmy. I told him I was calling to thank him for trying to save my little Bella. I began crying as I told him that not everyone would have done what he did. He asked me not to cry. I think it made him sad. He said he was going to work around 4:00 that afternoon, and as he made a left turn at a busy intersection, he saw a little dog with a dress run across the street before being hit by a truck. She rolled over and staggered to the curb. He didn't think the driver even saw her. Hearing him tell the story just broke my heart. It hurt to know that my poor little dog was hit and suffered.

Jimmy said he jumped out of his car, stopped the traffic by holding out his hand, picked her up, and held her in his arms on the way to his vet nearby. He said it was strange how the traffic stopped when he went to pick her up from the ground.

He said that Bella still appeared to be breathing the whole way to the vet's office. He held her in his arms the whole way. He parked in the front of the vet's office, ran inside, and frantically told them he had a dog that needed attention. He said there were other people in the waiting room. The vets tried to revive her but realized she had passed away from internal injuries. He said when he left the office he was crying and so were the people in the waiting room. When he told the story to people at work, they started crying, too.

Then he said something very comforting to me. He said that a strange thing happened that day. When he left the vet's office, his cell phone rang. There was no one on the line, and the number that showed on Caller ID was all zeros. He said that had never happened before, and he believed it was a sign that he had done the right thing.

I saw this as God calling. Zero is a universal symbol, representing the circle of life, completion.

It consoled me to know that Bella spent her last moments in the arms of someone so caring. I had hated the thought of her being scared and dying alone. When I was driving all over looking for her, I was asking my angels to help me find her. I guess they did. Of course I was angry that she did not make it, but because of this very kind and compassionate man, I was able to see her and make arrangements to bring her ashes home. Jimmy said he had a dog of his own and hoped someone would do the same thing for him. He did a good deed that day and certainly has good feng shui in my book. I now carry water, food, and a blanket in the back of my car in case I ever see an injured animal on the road, and I have told friends to do the same. I was so grateful to this man.

# Celebrating the Life

After my conversation with Jimmy, I felt better about hosting my dinner for the Chinese New Year. Most of the folks at the table knew what had happened, but some did not. I kept the conversation light.

With my friends around me, I dedicated the dinner to Bella and sent her wishes for a happy afterlife. Now, on my own I probably would have waited to do this dedication but my friends nudged me to get it out that evening. Everyone has their own time for this but at some point it is very healing to do this for your loved one. It helps you hold on to all the wonderful memories that will stay with you forever.

It is my spiritual belief that Bella has gone on to her next life to fulfill her purpose there. She was only meant to be with me for eight months. I even believe that her next life may be that of a human, perhaps a mother who will nurture a child herself. I dreamed about this one night. Bella taught me so much about love; she came into my life at a time when I needed that kind of nurturing and companionship. But I believe she learned a lot, as well.

Between relationships, I think I was lonely. I never realized how well a pet could fill that void. I looked forward to coming home to see her. I looked forward to our walks and outings. She was both roommate and friend. I know she was a dog, but she was also an important part of my life. I always loved the TV show *The Dog Whisperer*, and watched it many times before I got her. I learned a lot about healthy discipline, which I believe helped my relationship with Bella. I would see owners treat their dogs like humans and let their behaviors get out of hand. While I did pamper Bella, she was a well-behaved dog. She knew I was her pack leader and wanted to please me.

I liked the Dog Whisperer's techniques because he always talked about "energy." A dog can sense your energy without your words. I found this to be so true. Now, the show would say I should have trained her to obey my command of "Stop," which might have saved her life. This is something I regret. Training my future pets with this command will be a priority. I also know that no matter how well trained an animal is, if there is a trigger like a loud noise, a squirrel, a bird, etc. the chase or response is more important in that moment than your voice and any reprimand. Always have your pets on a leash if in an unsafe environment like a parking lot area. My lesson.

# Surrendering

I t is said that there is nothing to gain in life, nothing to strive for. We already have everything we need. The Universe is abundant; we have just set up blocks to receiving its gifts. There is no lack, no shortage. There is no such thing as a recession, as far as the Universe is concerned. All we need to do to live an abundant life is let go... let go of doubt, fear, and all those things blocking our prosperity.

In my feng shui practice, I set up each environment to make room for the Chi (abundance) to flow. It is up to each person to get out of his or her own way and allow what they want to come to them. Once unencumbered, you must take action. Getting rid of clutter is one way to do this, as it helps to remove stagnation and allows you to live your fullest life.

While there is an intricate system for understanding and working with Chi in the art of feng shui (like flying stars analyses, working with birthdates, etc.), the main part of my work involves helping people get rid of excess "stuff" to create movement in the important areas of their lives. Enhancing, energizing, or curing an elemental imbalance is the easy part for me as a consultant. The people who achieve the best results in feng shui are those who live simply, free of clutter, and open to abundance. These things are possible, whether you live in a small apartment or a large mansion. You can have beauty, elegance, and peace in any size space. Surrender the need to have things be a certain way and allow the universe to do its work.

It is a week since Bella's passing and I like to attend my Sunday night meditation group to see friends and clear my mind, but tonight I did not go. I feared that I would start crying if I silenced my mind. The room is usually so quiet, I didn't want to embarrass myself and the others by breaking down. Whenever I close my eyes, I relive that day in my mind and keep wishing I had it to do over. I was told by a friend who attended that they put Bella and me in a healing circle, and that many had been concerned about us. I am grateful for that group. They are my spiritual family.

Today I heard a spiritual teacher say, "If you don't need anything, you get everything." When I brought Bella into my life, I needed companionship and love. Rather than just having her with me as an addition to my life, I felt I needed her for my well-being. Wanting a dog and needing a dog are two different things. Need is what the Buddhists call *attachment*. When we accept that life is a journey and all its experiences are meant to teach us to be stronger spiritually, things flow in and out of our lives more harmoniously. We learn to accept what comes our way, whether good or bad. It doesn't mean we don't feel; it just means we don't hold on to things.

When we are in need of people or things, it makes it much harder when we lose them.

At first I went to a dark place, feeling like Bella was taken from me or that I was being punished somehow for past deeds. I needed to know that there was something new on the horizon for me. For every darkness, there is light. It is natural law. Perhaps I would have delayed my path because she kept me in my comfort zone.

When you want something too much, you hold on and resist the flow of life. Surrender the need to have things be different than they are. Desire, okay. Imagine, yes. Ask, yes. But then... let go. It is a challenge to do this in our world. That is why the daily practice of meditation and prayer have been so crucial for me to stay in the moment and centered.

My Chinese New Year dinner was good for me. I was able to let go of the old and begin the new. It was symbolic that something so precious to me died at the beginning of the new year, such an auspicious time. I have learned that we don't own anything. We can't take anything with us. We must treasure the moments we have in the Now. There were so many lessons I learned through this situation… was that what it was all about?

Being more mindful and letting go of attachments were two great lessons I learned, and continue to work on. I do get attached in relationships. I am human and care deeply. My ongoing spiritual teachings have taught me to have compassion and caring for others, but not to hold on for dear life.

Was Bella filling a void that I must heal within myself to be really happy? Is that why the pain was so great and my heart felt so broken? I began to explore these questions more deeply in my energy meditations and prayer work. Even after reaching a level of enlightenment where one can detach, feeling deeply and getting hurt when something meaningful occurs is part of being human. I have read that one is not enlightened; instead, there are moments of enlightenment. Bella enlightened me. She was a bodhisattva (an enlightened being, or angel).

# The Wisdom of the Tao

W hen bad things happen, we want answers. *Why me? Why did my pet leave me?*

Feng shui (pronounced "fung shway" in the West) is the 4,000-year old ancient art of harmonious placement. It is rooted in the Chinese philosophy called the Tao (pronounced "dow," like the "Dow Jones"). It is our connection with nature, the Universe, the cosmos, everything. Applied today, it can help people create more harmonious and prosperous lives for themselves. I have always felt that getting rid of clutter, making the space more open and sacred, and creating better flow was setting up the house so that God could visit anytime. With God, all things are possible.

When I talk to clients about keeping things organized, clean, and uncluttered to help improve flow, the approach is in line with sayings like "Cleanliness is next to Godliness," and "God is in the details." Whether you have a spiritual background or a strong belief system, it doesn't really matter as long as you feel you are connected to something greater than yourself (your ego). The Tao is the universal source (chi) that flows through everything.

Ancient Taoists were the quantum physicians of their time. They understood that everything was made of energy. My favorite Einstein quote is, "Nothing happens until something moves." In feng shui, we move things to create a different result. In my work I see clients with all kinds of life issues; I help them transform those issues into positive outcomes, which makes my work fulfilling. If moving things around helps them make their own connection to nature or God, I feel I have done my right work.

There are those who ask if practicing feng shui interferes with Christian principles? How can it? It is about connecting to the highest source there is, whether you call it Jesus, Buddha, God, Universe, Spirit, etc. If setting up your space allows for this then it has good feng shui. If you are spiritual and not religious, it is ultimately, all about the experience.

I see myself as a vessel of light energy, helping people find their own radiance. I love the quote, "We do not fear our inadequacies, but our greatness." This is something I have worked on in my own personal growth. As young girls we weren't taught to be proud of our accomplishments or to see ourselves as great. We were taught to be quiet, well-behaved, and tidy.

Notice how the word Tao has three letters. Ohm, the Sanskrit word meaning "highest support" and the merging of everything into one, has three letters, too. The zeroes that appeared on Jimmy's cell phone after he saved Bella were about the Tao, Ohm, our connection with everything, and the synchronization of life. Nothing in life is random.

According to the Tao, everything is pre-destined. If we are in harmony with the Tao, we can experience peace and happiness. If we resist, we find disharmony and chaos. Had I taken the news of the house I was living in being sold as something to flow with, rather than something to resist, the day's turn of events would have been totally different. That is not to say that I wouldn't have lost Bella, because what happened was meant to happen. You might ask why.

I believe it happened for my greater learning and to make me a stronger person. I also believe it was the Universe urging me on to something greater. It all resulted in my eventually owning the home, adopting my two new beloved pets and starting a pet support group

The Tao is made up of Yin and Yang; the balance of opposites, polarity, duality. This is the cycle of life. The black and white fish-looking images on the Tai Chi symbol are not two separate symbols, they are one

image that melds the two; Yin and Yang constantly moving back and forth, one continually changing into the other. It serves to remind us that in death there is life, and in life there is death. In sadness there is joy, and in joy there is sadness. We can't have one without the other. We can't experience one fully without knowing the other.

Bella brought me immense joy and then great sadness. Later there would be joy again. This is a reality. It must happen. It is inevitable unless we try to stop it. Though we are in an economic recession, things will improve. They have to, because for every down there is an up. This is nature, or the Tao, at work. Right now I want Bella back with me so I can hold her and play with her. My pain of missing her overrides any feelings of joy. But my faith tells me that, in time, this hurt will pass.

I was told by a good friend that Bella may be gone in the physical, but she is with me in spirit. Even though she is off to fulfill her new purpose, she and I have a bond that is eternal. She is always with me, like an angel on my shoulder. I have the tags she wore on the day she died, and I wear them close to my heart. I hold on to them in warmth and comfort, knowing it was all meant to be. Wearing something that belonged to your pet can help you feel close to their spirit. In feng shui, the closer that something is to you the more it will affect you.

I once worked with a client who wanted to do something to help her relationship. She had heard about feng shui and was interested in it. I share this story because she was also shocked by the loss of something important to her.

I met her at her home in Sedona, Arizona, while her husband was at work. The house had a cold feeling to it and felt transitional. There was no real heart to the home, or focus on any area other than the kitchen for eating. I asked to see the bedroom, as feng shui has some principles that can enhance relationships. Her bedroom had no warmth or energy for partnership. There was an ironing board set up in a corner, a bed, a nightstand, and no color on the walls. I suggested bringing things in pairs, adding some pink, creating a love altar in the relationship corner (in Black Hat Sect feng shui, this is the farthest right corner of the room).

I asked her to write her Intentions, noting what she really wanted from her marriage, and instructed her to place it in a red envelope on the bedside table. We manifest our dreams in our sleep, so having a reminder of what she desired close to her would be powerful. I suggested soft colors for the bedding and adding some romantic touches like candles. She was excited about the possibilities. I had met her husband and, while he was a nice and handsome man, he was not connecting with her at all. He was distant and cold, much like the feeling in the bedroom.

After some weeks had passed, I called my client to hear how things were going for her. She began crying on the phone and said that about a day after she'd made the changes, her husband had asked her for a divorce! Now, had I not been trained and experienced in feng shui, I would have felt I had failed her. I went to help her marriage, not end it. But I knew that it was not meant to be, and she had been holding on for dear life out of fear of being on her own. He had wanted out of the relationship for some time, and the movement we created caused him to act on it. The good news is, a couple of months later she met a friend who later turned into a love, and they have been together for years now. Her ex was soon in another relationship.

I liken the effects of feng shui to a water hose. It works, but when you step on the hose you shut off the flow and cause pressure to build. When we block something in life, we cause stagnation – but when we open things up we allow the truth to come forth and the natural order can reign. This client was not meant to stay with her husband; it was wrong for both her growth and his. Her desires were not in alignment with her life at the time, but now they are. She had to let go.

To clarify, feng shui does not create divorce. It is about harmony for all, and the way that manifests itself is up to the individual's personal destiny. These two people had a contract and that contract ended. It was time for a new spiritual contract. My contract with my little Bella had ended, too.

# Lessons

I have always been a believer that life is a school, and we are here to learn.

My life has not been easy. I think people who feel the loss of a pet deeply may also have had many painful experiences in their lives. I have gained wisdom from hard knocks, not from school, although my parents worked hard to give me a good education. I have not led a charmed life. There was stress and turmoil growing up in a lower middle class family with parents who both worked. They did the best they could with the knowledge they had at the time. I understood at a very young age that not everything is as it seems on the outside.

I was an introvert growing up, always an observer of life. My emotional life was turbulent and I was very sensitive. My difficult childhood made me a more compassionate person. I could have been bitter, angry, and cold about life, but my spiritual work has helped me move past those feelings and on to ones that are more positive. When Bella died, I was angry that such a beautiful thing in my life had been taken away from me. It had been a while since I had felt so content.

Being self-sufficient, financially abundant, empowered, spiritually connected, and happy were all the things that I was teaching in my work. It is said that you teach what you need to learn. Not having had any real losses like this in my life up to now, the Universe was going to teach me that life lesson too.

Loss comes in many forms and I have experienced several of them. I have lost a job, which devastated me at the time. I had no savings and many bills when I lost that job, so fear gripped me. I got a divorce and, although I was ready for the marriage to end, I suffered from post-traumatic relationship syndrome for years. I had waited a long time to get married; while most of my friends were married in their 20s, I married at 32. I believed I had made the right choice, so when it ended I felt like a failure.

Looking back at my life, it seems like I experienced a lot of these things in reverse. When I wanted financial freedom, I didn't have any money. When I wanted a secure place to live, I was forced to move. When I wanted a loving pet, the one I found was taken from me. What I later learned was that all these wants were based on fear. Fear of not having money, not having a place to live, not having LOVE.

I remember once listening to a spiritual author who wrote that if you ask the Universe for something you will get its polar opposite. Again, here is the Tao and its duality. One experience really brought this principle home for me:

I had a hysterectomy in 2001. It was invasive and threw me into menopause early. My stomach was cut across from one side to the other, so I had a very long incision. I lost a lot of blood during the surgery, which made me anemic. I also had a large benign tumor on my uterus the size of a grapefruit, according to my surgeon.

I understand from mind-body medicine that fibroid tumors come from past hurts, not nurturing one's creative side, or being too much like a man (too *yang*). Well, in my corporate job of 18 years, I'd had to be more *yang* (strong, assertive, aggressive) to survive. I was the only female on an all-male leadership team and they didn't like it. I had worked hard to excel, leaving little time for me. When I resigned from my job I needed a lot of rest. I decided to take care of my health.

After the surgery, I could not walk around for four weeks. On the fourth week, I went to the nearby grocery store. I had cabin fever and the doctor said it was good to walk some. Feeling low energy from the anemia, I took my time. I walked slowly to my car, hanging on to the grocery basket. It was a hot summer day in Memphis, Tennessee, so I was a bit sluggish. It was about 5:30 pm when a man approached me at my car door to tell me I had dropped my pen. When I looked down, he pushed me, grabbed my purse, and ran off. He didn't hurt me but I was startled. I screamed but no one came around, even though it was still daylight and everyone could see.

Some people just stared. They might not have known what was going on, but they could have asked. The security guard was nowhere to be found. I went inside the store as fast as I could, where my bank happened to have a branch. Interesting that I would be at a store with my bank onsite… here is synchronicity, once again revealing itself to me.

I was frantic as I asked the teller to call the police and put a hold on my ATM card. I had just received a new pin number for my ATM and had not had a chance to put it away. It was in the purse they had taken.

The robbers went to several ATM machines in minutes, the gas station for gas, charged on my credit cards, and used my bank checks.

At this time in my life I was going through some more changes. I had just sold my beautiful home, had moved in with a friend (a situation that was not working out), had surgery, and was building my business while looking for part-time work. When this happened I asked myself, "What next?"

When I set my Intentions at the beginning of each year, I usually ask to improve some area of my life. This year I had asked to learn generosity. While I felt I was already a generous person, I wanted to be more grounded in it since it is the foundation for prosperity. But now here I was, being robbed of my abundance. What gives?

On the day of the mugging, I handled the necessary details by asking the teller at the bank to put a hold on my checks and calling all the credit card companies to close my accounts. After a good night's sleep, I told the Universe, "It's okay. I guess the guy who robbed me needed the money more than I did." That thought shifted something huge in me. I felt a weight lift and was hit with the realization that I would be taken care of. A short time after that, all of my accounts were restored at no cost to me. The bank and credit card companies wrote off the losses. I remained grateful that I had not been hurt or killed during the mugging.

This attitude of forgiveness did not take any responsibility off of me or the mugger. I was not totally well that day since I was still recuperating from surgery. I was not as alert as I usually am. I could relate to how vulnerable elderly, sick, or disabled people might feel on a daily basis. Weaker energies get preyed upon. I was not walking with my head up or paying attention, and I did not put my ATM card in a safe place as soon as I received it. We are still responsible for our lives. I feel we are co-creators in this wonderful Universe. We need to take the lessons from things that happen to us whether they are good or bad. It is not about being punished, it is about learning and growing. Since that time, I have been much more aware of what I carry in my purse, watch when I get into my car, etc. It is not from fear, but from being mindful that all things are sacred, especially our lives.

This all happened right after I had resigned from a hectic corporate life of non-stop travel and stress. I told the Universe I just needed a break. I speak to the universe on a regular basis. I was so tired; I remember saying that all I wanted to do after I resigned was sleep non-stop for a month. I went to an ayurvedic physician who determines your body constitution from your pulse. It is a fascinating medicine. She then recommends foods, supplements, or a regime to bring you back into balance. She told me that I needed none of her remedies. To start, she recommended I spend a month on an island alone with no cellphone! I got the message. In medical sales, my role was to observe the surgeries where my products were being used, to act as a resource for the surgeons, to further develop those relationships, and to make sure the product was being used as it was intended. I had to be in the Operating Room by 7:30 am for surgeries, so I had been getting up at 4:30 am for 15 years.

When I took this long-needed break, my body needed work. While my money had been returned to me after the mugging, I was still not in the best place financially. Soon, though, I had some good consulting jobs, my feng shui practice was growing, and I'd found a beautiful place to live, a relationship, good friends, time with family… and then Bella.

I had no idea what experiences would come after my request to learn generosity, or what would happen after I let go of my anger. Abundance flowed.

# Transitions are Necessary

osing a dear pet had me facing transitions in my life. I remember the day I resigned from my corporate career. I had been wanting a change for a while. After years of excessive traveling, I was tired. It had been glamorous in the beginning because everywhere I went was new to me, but after doing it for many years it got old. While I loved my job, I wanted a change and some rest. I needed more balance in my life.

I was the firstborn child and the only female, so responsibility was my middle name. I remember the day I made the decision to leave my stable job with good pay of 14 years. It was a pivotal moment. I was at a sales meeting in Toronto, Canada, and my boss told me that he was promoting someone over me who had only been with the company a couple of years. I had been there 12 years, I was a consistent top producer bringing in millions in revenue, had great reviews from my team and co-workers, and was on the sales leadership team – yet he had chosen to mentor the new guy for some higher position.

After hearing the news, I went upstairs to get ready for a dinner meeting. I was in tears, out of exhaustion from work and from the frustration of watching yet another man get special favors just because he was "one of the guys." Over the years I had seen many times that the good old boy network was alive and well in this company. Because they were privately held, they got away with it. Few women who were strong and assertive in the company lasted very long. There was ongoing sexual harassment, but it was usually settled out of court so the company looked like they had a good track record when it came to diversity. Most of those harassed women left the company. I was just tired of it all. I wondered if the male sales leaders would want their daughters treated that way.

When I got to my room, I fell to my knees and prayed. I asked God to give me a sign, to tell me what to do. I was so angry I wanted to quit right there on the spot. I wanted to leave but did not want to make a bad decision. I am a pretty rational person.

Then something amazing happened. I turned on the TV while getting ready for dinner, and *Oprah* was on. I was a longtime Oprah fan and either recorded or watched her show daily. I was even in her audience back in the 80s. On this day, the topic was "Go for the dream, not the money." What synchronicity! I had just asked God for an answer and minutes later this message appeared. The guests included women who had left their high paying jobs to do what they loved. I took that as my sign and started putting the ball in motion to resign. I do believe the Universe answers our prayers.

It took me eight months from that day to leave, because I had to be sure. I went to therapy with a woman who was very spiritual (from the Zen Buddhist tradition). The fear of leaving a great paycheck behind was very strong; I had worked so hard to get to my pay level. No one in my family had ever made that kind of money. It was an accomplishment. It was my security. What if I didn't make it? How would I survive? I didn't personally know anyone in my life who had walked away from a six-figure salary career to no job, just a dream. My therapist never gave me advice or steered me into leaving. She just asked great questions about my desires and dreams.

Now, I could have taken a leave of absence for a few months or even a year; my job would still have been there for me because I was in such good standing – but I felt my soul was starving. I also felt that nothing in the company would ever change. I knew I would be coming back to the same circumstances. So I left, for good.

I believe we get messages from our higher self/spirit to confirm that we are going in the right direction – but we must pay attention and be open to receiving them. I had a strong affirmation/sign just a few weeks later. Before I left, the stock in my company had been at the highest level it had been in all the years I worked there. When you leave, the stock price and shares due to you are based on that date.

With the help of an astrologer, I picked a date to resign. One week after I left, the stock price dropped to its lowest in history! I was grateful I was able to leave with a great stock price to roll over into a new retirement account. It was if the Universe was saying, "Go ahead. You will be okay."

I only had enough savings to last me two years, yet here I am 12 years later, still on my own. I have had some financial struggles but always seem to move through them. For me leaving was not only about following my passion, but also to learn some of life's lessons about faith and courage. I felt like someone leaving a wealthy family, cutting herself off from the family fortune and forging ahead with nothing more than a backpack and little money. It is not for everyone. That kind of risk takes a strong, adventurous person, and I didn't think I was one of those. All I had was faith in something greater than me, my higher self, Source, and I knew it wanted me to be happy.

*The Course in Miracles* is one of my favorite texts and it says, "If you knew who stood beside you at every moment, you would never have any fear," referring to Jesus. I have come to realize it is this faith that has kept me going. It has been my strongest resource. While I consider myself a highly spiritual person, I do not call myself religious, much to my parent's dismay. I was raised Catholic, attending Catholic school from Kindergarten to eighth grade without ever missing a day (except for three weeks in the third grade, when I had the measles). I went to Mass every day during those years.

I am grateful for that background; it gave me my profound belief in God and the angels/saints. I follow Christ's teachings. I have studied the Bhagavad Gita, a very spiritual text on which Mahatma Gandhi based his life's work. I meditate once a week with the Zen Buddhists. While I am not a Buddhist, I study and practice Buddha's teachings. I studied these faiths as I believe there are many pathways to the truth.

I find Buddha and Christ's teachings to be so similar: Be loving, kind, and compassionate to all living beings. I have always felt that all religions lead to the same place, by different roads. For me, this approach leaves the door open to experience so much more than what one teaching or doctrine can offer. Had I the chance to go back to school, I might have majored in comparative religious studies; I am fascinated by how people came to believe what they did back in ancient times.

Wherever you are today, know that the transition you are going through will move you into a happier place again. Sometimes these changes come from the choices we make, like me leaving my corporate job, or from losing a pet unexpectedly like I did. In the end, it is the soul's purpose to move us forward in life. We must allow our lost loved ones to do the same.

My spirituality has helped me throughout a life hit hard by challenges and difficult circumstances. In feng shui astrology, there is a system called the 9 Star Ki. Based on your birth date, a predominant element is considered your core nature. Mine is the number 8 Mountain, which is an earth element. I am a person who gains wisdom through experiences. I know this to be true. While I have made some bad decisions in my life, I have also done many good things and been given many gifts. I have learned from the bad experiences and allowed them to make me stronger as a person. I know now that my boss' choice to promote someone else was the spirit's way of sending me off to do other things. I simply wasn't meant to stay with that company.

What kept me going – and still does – is all the insight my journey has brought me. I am a seeker of knowledge, in any way I can get it. I look at everything with the eyes of a sage, to gain even more wisdom. I find life to be profoundly meaningful. My purpose is not to be great or tell people how to live their lives, but to find deeper meaning and richness in all that life has to offer me. On the day I left my job, I told the Universe I wanted more time for myself to re-charge, be more in balance, have fun, play, and laugh. And then I found feng shui.

No other job, career path, or hobby ever interested me enough to leave a six-figure salary. When I had my home feng shui-ed by a teacher/practitioner and saw the remarkable changes in my life and career that resulted, I knew I wanted to share it with others. My own feng shui story is pretty remarkable.

When I was living in Memphis, Tennessee, I could not find anyone in my part of the country who knew anything about feng shui. When I did find a teacher he was in New York, his services were pricey, and my pay was only average at the time. Still, we spoke by phone and he offered to help me. He asked me to send him pictures of all the rooms in my house. He instructed me to pick one life area I wanted to enhance, so we could make the most of the consultation.

During this time I was unhappy with my career path. I was doing all the right things, working hard, but not getting pay raises or promotions. I had already feng shui-ed my home the best I knew how, based on one of the only books on the market at the time: *Interior Design with Feng Shui* by Sarah Rossbach. It was based on Black Hat Sect feng shui, which is rooted in Tibetan Buddhism and uses many spiritual cures which really interested me because of my spiritual background. I had dog-eared the book and highlighted all the pages. I had moved some furniture around so the rooms flowed better; I added lucky bamboo on my desk for longevity; put some red candles in the South part of my office to enhance fame and reputation; hung a round crystal over my desk for clarity; and added a water feature for prosperity. What I liked about Black Hat Sect was that there were so many different cures or remedies for things. For my consultation, I decided to focus on my career, so I waited for the expert's call in my home office.

He said there were a few things he had noticed from my photos, but he was mostly concerned with my front door. I was surprised at that, since I thought we were working on my office and I did not send him any photos of my front door. With a focus on improving my career, the office made sense to me. He asked if I used the front door. I said no. He asked why. I told him it was stuck, so I just used the garage entrance. He asked me how long it had been stuck, and I said about two years. He then asked me how long my career had been stuck. I thought back to the last time I'd had a pay raise, and it had been two years! At this point I was very curious.

He said, "In feng shui, your front door represents the mouth of Chi, where the energy enters your space. It enters through your architectural front door. Yours happens to be in the Career Gua (area) of the Bagua Map. This is a map or grid we use to define life areas in your space." The Feng Shui Bagua Map can be found in any feng shui book or on the Internet. It is an octagon-shaped map showing 8 directions, the 5 elements with their corresponding colors, life areas and their meanings, body parts, and numbers. It is based on one of the oldest divination tools, called the I-ching. The Universe is so expansive, this is a way of bringing it closer to us. The map can be used on your home, a room, the land your house sits on, a city, your car, your desk, etc. It is meant to help organize your life, applying attention to areas you might be neglecting.

Most of my clients today love understanding the Bagua, because it allows them to keep their feng shui updated and maintain good energy in their spaces. It serves as a reference chart. I had thought I understood the Bagua before the consultant called, but more was to be learned. He said, "By using your garage, you are taking a circuitous route to your career – not a direct line." The interesting thing is that I had done everything the feng shui book had suggested, and read all the pages carefully, but I had missed that one principle! He said, "My advice to you is to get your front door fixed and begin using it."

He gave me some other cures or remedies as they are called, like writing Intentions and placing some mirrors in my garage to avoid blocking the energy flow whenever I did use that entrance. Mirrors have been called the "aspirin" in feng shui. They are used for so many issues. They can either repel, expand, or contract energy. Due to their reflective nature they represent the water element. In feng shui, water is money, abundance, and flow. By driving into my garage and seeing a flat wall when I arrived home would be considered a block to my career. By placing mirrors there it opened up the view, symbolic of opportunities, expansion in my career and money flow. I placed a pair for the balance of yin and yang in my life.

Intentions are extremely important. If you don't know what you want, you won't recognize it when it comes to you. Asking the Universe for what we want but acting as though we already have it is key to effective feng shui. When writing your Intentions, it is important to always state them in the present tense and then show gratitude for the ones already working in your life.

An example of an Intention for me was, "My career is going well and I am being paid well for my efforts. This and more is now happening in my life. Thank you God, or Universe." I have learned throughout my practice that being grateful for all that I have and that is working now, keeps things flowing well. Right after I hung up with the consultant, I went to find someone to repair the front door. I wasn't a true believer yet, but figured it couldn't hurt to follow his instructions and see what happened.

The first business I picked out of the phone book offered to come over right away. I was home from a business trip working on administrative tasks, so it was a great time to do this. A nice man and his young son arrived and began working on my beautiful wood door, with its side panels of leaded glass in a fleur de lis pattern. They took the heavy wood door off its hinges, put it on a saw horse, and began to work on leveling it. The house had settled, which was why the door was stuck. They repaired it in no time. When I pulled out my checkbook the man said, "Oh no, you don't owe us anything. We were the ones who put your door on in the first place." As it turned out, he was also the city's mayor. He had a door company as a side job. Now I was really beginning to see things unfold… not only did I get my door repaired for free, but by the mayor of the city! I thanked him profusely and implemented some of the feng shui consultant's other changes.

Within a couple of days I received a call inviting me to apply for a job in another division of my company, a job more profitable than the one I was in. Had it not been for this experience, I might have passed on that opportunity, seeing it as too much of a risk. But instead, I saw it as movement and energy flowing in the direction of my dreams. I was welcomed into that other division with open arms, and received more pay raises and promotions in two years than I had seen in the previous ten!

During the next two years, I saw constant growth and progressed from sales representative to national sales trainer and mentor to over 30 people in the company. I later became the only woman in sales leadership, a position I still held at the time I resigned in 2000.

My great experience with feng shui in my career motivated me to pursue it as a profession, attending training with many masters in both the U.S. and China. Years later, I have time to enjoy things like friends, family, and pets. I am able to create each day in any way I choose. Creating is an important part of life. I feel tremendous freedom working for myself and that has real value.

Two weeks before I resigned, my boss called to tell me how much he valued my work. He informed me that I was up for another raise. I thanked him without telling him I was leaving. I had firmly made up my mind and did not want to be talked out of it. After the call, I felt the Universe was really testing me, throwing more money at me to see if I would I go for the dream or the money. I went for the dream.

While my transition from a corporate life to one of an entrepreneur was challenging financially, it gave me inner strength. But, like the loss of Bella, I actually grieved the loss my corporate career. Even though the decision to leave was mine, I missed all that it could have been. I felt I could have made a real difference there; as the only woman in sales leadership at the time, I could have brought more harmony and balance to the team and the corporation, as well. I could have served as an example for other up-and-coming leaders. I guess it was just not my calling to do so. I missed my colleagues and the friends I had made over the years. Just like I wondered what my future would hold after I lost Bella, my new life was unknown. This was a similar feeling I had when I divorced.

When my husband and I divorced, we both knew we needed to go our separate ways. Still, I went to therapy for help with the transition. When he moved out, I kept really busy, so busy that I never stopped, constantly on the move, constantly running. I could not sleep and when I did, I had nightmares. I told this to my therapist and the first thing out of his mouth was, "What are you running from?" I broke down and really cried. I had not cried much over the divorce; I was so frustrated and angry with my ex by the time it ended, I just felt relieved when it was over. I told the therapist, "I don't know why I am crying, I wanted out of the marriage as much as he did." The therapist looked right at me and so profoundly said, "Your tears are for the loss of the dream." That statement hit me hard and stayed with me for years. He was so right. I wanted a good partnership, mate, marriage, and family, but it eluded me. I was sad about that and the fact that I was alone again.

My nightmares were about the unknown. While I have always been self-sufficient and independent, I struggled with loneliness and longed for real love. I attracted men incapable of real intimacy. I had my own work to do first. I needed to love myself before I could really love another. My time with my ex-husband taught me this.

When Bella passed, I grieved the loss of my dream of her in my life. I had envisioned doing so many things with her, and they were not going to be. This is why we must focus on all the fun times we had with our pets and the great lives that we provided for them.

# Blaming Ourselves

When Bella came into my life, she allowed me to be vulnerable. No one was watching. I could love and hold her all day if I wanted. She was always there waiting for me. She was happy and playful. She didn't judge me or make me feel confined.

Sure, there was a level of responsibility in having her. I had to make work and relationship decisions around her. Who would watch her while I was away at work or had to travel? I remember when I first brought her home. She was just 8 weeks old and cried all night long in her crate for two weeks straight. I would take her out about every two to four hours to pee. In her crate I kept a warm blanket and a stuffed toy, along with a towel with her mother's scent on it. I tried to make her first few days in a strange environment feel as secure as possible. She missed her mom.

I would sometimes fall asleep at work, after those late nights with Bella. I wondered if I had made the right decision in getting a new puppy. It's hard work. I can understand what older parents of newborns must go through. She was distracting me from my career tasks. But months later she had become such a big part of my life that I could not imagine having felt that way. When I lost her I remembered that time and felt guilty for having those thoughts. Since I believe your thoughts have a strong impact on your reality maybe they contributed to her going away. Did feeling she was a burden put an energy in motion that ultimately led to her death?

Blaming ourselves is one way of staying stuck. It is trying to control the situation. If I blame myself, then it can all make sense. But mystical, spiritual events don't make sense; they are not supposed to. Life is a mystery. Just when we think we have it figured out, we get trumped again. I don't say this to be negative. One thing I have noticed in my life is that you can be happy, but you can never stop the lessons from coming.

When tragedy hits, we can let it devastate us or we can see it as a spiritual experience from which we will grow. Being mindful each day and looking at life's experiences as blessings can help us strengthen our connection to Source, to God, the Universe, ourselves.

My time with Bella kept me from thinking about my path. It seemed too hard to figure out my purpose, my best career move, my job, my role. It was easier to focus on her than to fulfill my own life's destiny when I wasn't even sure what that was. I now understand that she was part of my path. She was here for a short time to fill my life with joy and fun, things that I had been lacking. Now that time was over and we were both meant to move on to bigger and better things. I would find joy in other things, but still carry her spirit with me in my heart always.

# Pray Your Way to Peace

When I came home after the accident, I needed to pray. I felt weak. I asked God to help me through the situation. Call in your angels or guides to surround you when you are sad or afraid. In my life, I have found that they do show up quickly when asked – but you have to ask.

I took out my beautifully carved metal Tibetan prayer wheel that I had bought during my feng shui training trip to China. Encased in the bell are rolls of paper with millions of prayers written on them in an ancient language known as Sanskrit. I'm not sure how the bell makers got all those prayers in there, but I could feel its energy.

I once sat next to a Buddhist monk on an airline flight from Sedona to Phoenix, Arizona, and he was spinning his large hand-made wooden prayer wheel. As I watched, mesmerized, he told me that when you spin the wheel it is as if a thousand Buddhas are praying for you. He had just been to see the Dalai Lama at a conference. I felt safe sitting next to him, despite the bumpy flight.

The night that I lost Bella, I spun my little prayer wheel over the special altar I'd created for her. I used the beautiful O Mani Pad Me Hum chant, which in Tibetan Buddhism calls for the attention of divine beings representing compassion. I cried while I chanted. I walked through the house saying the chant and expressing any feelings that came up. I apologized again to Bella, told her I missed her, said I wanted her to be happy, and asked for healing for her and myself. This purging of emotions was very healing for me.

Parents who have lost children to accidents they feel responsible for must feel inconsolable. An exercise like this may help. It is something they can do on their own when they really need to break down and let it all out.

One of my really favorite prayer books is *Illuminata*, by Marianne Williamson. In the beautiful little gold and burgundy book, she has powerful prayers for most of life's issues. Her prayer about Death really consoled me. I read it that night and many nights afterwards to help me sleep I always put Bella's name in it. Here are a few lines…

*Please take the soul and spirit of my dear Bella into the sweetest corner of your mind, the most tender place in your heart, that she, and I, might be comforted.*
*For now she has gone, and I pray, dear God, for the strength to remember she has not gone far.*

*I surrender to you my pain.*

*Please take care of your servant, my dear Bella who has passed.*

*And please dear Lord, take care of me.*

Place your own loved one's name into the prayer.

# Get Support

$\mathcal{J}$ went to a grief support group at church after my divorce. Since I had wanted the divorce and had already been to therapy, I hadn't been sure I really needed it, but my church was offering it so I decided to go just in case I was missing something. It was so powerful. While I was able to work through some other feelings, I found myself more affected by the ways others in the group were handling their own grief.

One woman cried the whole time, but had no idea why. She cried while other people were talking and when the facilitator was speaking. The facilitator kept asking her questions to help her uncover her sadness. She said she had nothing to cry about and didn't understand why she couldn't stop. She was so shut down emotionally that it took the whole day for her to realize what she needed.

I knew I needed support when Bella passed, so within that first week I called a support group sponsored by the Austin Humane Society for grieving pet owners. Reaching out at a time like this is important to healing. The group consisted of people who were in the process of losing their pets to illnesses and others who had already lost their pets months earlier. It was too soon for me and I was too raw to be there, but I did get some comfort. I needed more alone time before a group like that would be helpful.

Be sure to find a group as soon as you feel ready. Don't go it alone. These groups are confidential and anonymous, and sometimes it is easier to express your emotions to others who are experiencing or have experienced similar circumstances. It is also often easier to express deep pain to strangers than to those close to you, especially those you feel might not be able to handle it. When we are in deep pain, we feel extremely vulnerable and need support.

On their website, I found a most beautiful prayer that was so comforting to me. I read it every night for days.

## The Rainbow Prayer

As much as I loved the life we had
and all the times we played,
I was so very tired and knew my
time on earth would fade.

And running through the meadows
as far as the eye could see
Were animals of every sort as healthy as could be!

I wanted to reach out to you, to tell you I'm alright.

So whenever you need to find me, we're never far apart
If you look beyond the Rainbow and
listen with your heart.....

# Synchronicity of Life

Synchronization is a word I love. Webster defines it as:

*the coincidental occurrence of events and especially psychic events (as similar thoughts in widely separated persons or a mental image of an unexpected event before it happens) that seem related but are not explained by conventional mechanisms of causality —used especially in the psychology of C. G. Jung*

This is what we grew up calling coincidences. I have since learned there is no such thing. Everything is connected. It is the Tao in action. When my brother, who lives out of state, heard the news about Bella, he sent me a picture of a beautiful rainbow. A friend had sent it to him, not knowing of my situation. When I opened his e-mail I just thought it was a pretty rainbow and thoughtful that he sent it. But later that night when I read the rainbow poem for the first time, it had much more meaning.

My brother said when he heard the news about Bella he felt my pain all the way from Boston. He cried for her. Families have psychic connections like this all the time. Grief can bring families together and open hearts that are often closed. My mother, who has never been a pet lover, cried. She said, "I was surprised, it was the first time I ever cried over a dog." She later revealed that she felt a loss because Bella was like part of the family.

My mom and dad never had pets growing up. In lower income Hispanic families, if you had dogs they stayed outside. They were considered dirty. I have noticed that in poverty-stricken third world countries dogs are often kept outside, unkempt, and not considered part of the family. It is all people can do to feed themselves much less an animal. In America dogs are domesticated, treated like part of the family – like royalty, in some cases. Even my mom's friends cried. They didn't know me that well, but Bella's passing brought up their own grief or feelings of potential loss.

# The Grief of Others

J read a passage this morning that comforted me.

*We Are of the Same Nature*

*After you wake up you probably open the curtains and look outside. You may even like to open the window and feel the cool morning air with the dew still on the grass. But is what you see really "outside"? In fact, it is your own mind. As the sun sends its rays through the window, you are not just yourself. You are also the beautiful view from your window. You are the way of understanding and love. Before passing away, the Buddha told his disciples, "Only my physical body will pass away. My Dharma body will remain with you forever." In Buddhism, the word has come to mean "the essence of all that exists." All phenomena--the song of a bird, the warm rays of the sun, a pet--are manifestations of the Dharmakaya. We, too, are of the same nature as these wonders of the universe.*

- Thich Nhat Hanh, *Present Moment, Wonderful Moment*

Believing that Bella is with me in spirit and that we are one helps me feel better, even though I miss her touch and sweet face looking up at me. I want to go for my daily walk with her, brush her soft shiny hair, play ball with her. Does the missing ever go away?

I had donated a feng shui consultation to the Austin Humane Society for a Valentine's Day silent auction. I would help the winning bidder set up a nice space in their home for their pet. Like humans, pets feel energy and need to sleep in places that feel good and are healthy. I had been planning to take Bella to the fundraiser, where she could be around other dogs. Without her, I did not feel up to going – but I sent the gift certificate for the auction.

I then had to call my vet, because Bella had been scheduled for her spaying. A vet technician answered my call. When I told him I could not bring Bella in because she had been killed, he said he was sorry. I never heard from the office or my vet after that. I thought a card or a call would have been appropriate, since I had been in there so many times and had even given them a couple of pictures of Bella that they had posted on their wall. Needless to say, I never went back there again. It takes so little to make a difference in people's lives. Businesses fail from lack of good customer service and caring. They lose out on referrals and good clients.

# The Gift of Deep Listening

I found that talking about the situation and being heard was important. A dear friend invited me to her home, and on that visit she let me share. She also showed me a video of her mom's assisted living center, which happened to have a "Pet Pal" program. A Yorkie larger than Bella would come every day to visit the seniors who could not move around very well. She brought joy to them. I had planned to do this with Bella. Just spending time with my friend who listened to me was so comforting.

I shared with her a time I remembered over Christmas holidays, walking with my brother and Bella in a very beautiful wooded area in San Antonio, Texas. It was a cold day and nestled in the woods was a nursing home. We went inside to warm up. This was a couple of months prior to her death, and due to the holidays the nursing home was decorated beautifully. Because hospitals don't usually allow dogs, my brother tried to hide Bella under his jacket so no one would see us while we made our way through the place and out the back to avoid the cold for a few moments. But before I could make my way out the door, some nurses at a center station called out in a kidding manner, "Can we hold your dog while you walk around?" I laughed and said, "I don't think so!" But I did walk back in and let them hold her. Some of the older residents stopped to pet her. I remember these moments well.

In speaking to people during this difficult time, I have noticed that many have grieved the loss of their pets. In listening to their stories I am learning more about family and friends than I knew before. My brother said he lost a dog and cried for about two weeks whenever he visited the area where they used to walk. My next door neighbor said she was walking her dog on a leash and a large dog that was loose in the neighborhood ran across the yard and attacked her dog and killed it. She now fears large dogs. Another friend said she was babysitting a friend's dog when it got loose, ran away and got hit by a car. She felt so guilty.

I've also noticed that others often share their grief when I share mine. Sometimes it's not even a pet. At funerals, I've always wondered why some would cry over people they really didn't know very well. I understood that they might be feeling sadness for the family or reliving some memories of the deceased, but to really break down over a relationship that was not very close was interesting to me. I came to understand that they were grieving their own losses, experiencing feelings that came up from being around other's sadness.

Perhaps they were not allowed to express their grief or be listened to during their time of sadness. Many family members don't allow the grief-stricken person to be sad; instead, they do all they can to hide any memories of that person. Had they allowed the person to talk about their feelings and really be heard, the process of healing would have begun allowing the person to feel more at peace.

In time, with grief work, the missing may lessen but continuing to talk about it as needed will help. Hopefully the memories change to joy, not sadness. Four years later, I still tear up when I hear a particular song or pass by the area where Bella died. It doesn't bring me down, though. Instead, it reminds me of her. I think she wants me to know that she's okay, she wants me to remember her. I feel her spirit within me. If I want to connect with her I put on John Denver music. I played his greatest hits CD in the car several months before she died.

Your loved one will let you know how they want to reach you. You will just know. It could be a bird you have never seen that shows up on your windowsill, or the pets in your home staring at something on your shoulder. They see something you don't. If you want, be open, and you will feel your loved one close.

Don't be concerned about the when or the how. Just be open.

It is four days now since my Bella passed away. She was scheduled to be in a doggie fashion show. We had just been in a really cool dog store a couple of weeks ago; it carried everything from dog sunglasses to bomber jackets. The owner said she had just the right thing for Bella to model, and asked if she could be in the show. It was decided that she would wear a soft pink, plush doggie bathrobe with house slippers. Can you imagine? Even I thought it was a bit much for a pet, but it was so funny and cute, I was looking forward to seeing her model it.

I called the store the day after she died to tell the owner. I was glad no one answered and I could just leave a message. She called me back and left me a nice message of condolence. I could tell on the phone that she really heard me. She was upset and sad, as well. I know Bella would have been one of the stars of the show. I will always regard that store owner highly for her kindness, and to this day still refer many people to her stores.

# Colors Can Heal

It has been proven that color has energy. In feng shui, we wear colors to either give us energy or help us feel more balanced. You will sometimes see powerful businessmen wearing red ties for energy and success. I often dressed little Bella in pink. At the time I didn't do this to heal anything but now looking back, I can see it more clearly. In feng shui, pink is the color of love. I was healing my own issues with self-love by having her in my life.

There are seven spiritual energy centers in the body; they are called the Chakras. Feng shui has been called "acupuncture for the home," since our work involves energizing stagnant or blocked areas in the home. These areas have corresponding body areas, which can be healed with good feng shui. This is what makes it a fascinating healing art.

Chakras come from the Indian tradition and relate to color. Each Chakra is represented by a color, which evokes that particular energy. Why do we wear dull or black colors when grieving? Because we want to retreat within, not be bothered, feel protected. In that state, high energy colors make us feel too much.

Here are the Chakra colors as they relate to the areas of the body:

7) **Gold/Yellow** represents the Crown, or spiritual center, and the area above the head. It is sometimes seen as white.

6) **Violet** is for the Third Eye, or Intuition (middle of the forehead).

5) **Blue** is for the Throat, which represents communication.

4) **Green** represents the Heart.

3) **Yellow** is for the Solar Plexus (navel area) and represents survival.

2) **Red/Orange** is for the Root Chakra, or sexual energy.

1) **Yellow** is for the Sacrum area, or tail, and represents support.

I use crystals in my Reiki healing practice to help balance the Chakras. Balancing the Chakras makes a person feel at peace and leaves them feeling more grounded than when they came in for the session. If they have a particular issue, I place a crystal on the body area that needs healing, with the color for that Chakra. For example, if a person is having trouble making a decision, I might place an amethyst or purple crystal on the person's forehead while performing my energy work. This helps to open up that person's intuition. For a person who is grieving, a green crystal on the heart helps comfort them. All healings are done with the intention of helping the person at the specific level needed.

This is something you can do at home right away, if you find out about a tragedy. Place your hands over your heart breathing deeply, asking your guides to help you through it, and to comfort you. The healing will begin immediately. Later, when you feel ready, seek a body worker to help you through your process. Reiki, massage, rolfing, acupuncture, and healing touch are just a few examples of body work. We store emotions in our tissues and, with the help of a body worker, you can feel a great sense of relief.

Many compassionate healers offer tremendous emotional support for those in need. To find one, ask your friends for their referrals, or go to www.reiki.org and locate a practitioner near you.

For healing on the go, you can wear the colors of the Chakras by way of jewelry or clothing. Wear a pink rose quartz crystal to nurture yourself during a difficult time. It has the healing properties of love.

# Colors and Elements

In feng shui, we use colors in the home that correspond to the five elements in nature. They help provide balance to the areas of our lives that need healing and attention. It is said that the right proportion of the five elements in a space will create good balance.

Balance is a strong word. If we were in total balance, we would be dead. There would be nothing to do. Balance is ever-changing, like the Tao. We can only become more balanced. That is what we, as practitioners, endeavor to do in feng shui.

The five elements in nature are Wood, Fire, Earth, Metal and Water. Each has corresponding colors and energies:

**Green for Wood** New Beginnings/Opportunities; Health

**Red for Fire** Prosperity; High Energy; Passion

**Blue/Black for Water** Introspection; Intuition

**Pastels/Whites for Metallics** Manifesting or Creating

**Pink/Earthtones for Earth** Love; Nurturing Oneself and Others.

On days when I wear certain colors, I often check in to see how I am feeling that day. I have noticed myself wearing a lot of black lately. Black is the color for the water element; it can represent introspection and sensitivity, or deep mystery. I like to wear green for physical health when I feel under the weather and red for vitality on days when I feel tired. If you are just coming out of deep grief and want to feel better, you might try adding a touch of color to your wardrobe. Even on days when I feel some sadness, I make an effort to wear a bright cheery color somehow. I might add a colorful scarf, piece of jewelry, colorful lipstick, purse, or another accessory. Men can do the same with a tie, sweater, vest, or cap. Just adding a simple touch of color can help restore balance and lift Chi. In feng shui, adorning ourselves means nurturing ourselves.

Most of Bella's outfits were pink to show off her pretty dark hair and the fact that she was a girl. Still, I was amazed that some people would ask if she was a boy or a girl, even with a bow in her hair! I also dressed her in red sometimes. The day she died, though, she was in a pink polka-dotted dress with a pink bow in her hair and a pink collar. At the time, I did not consciously think of the symbolic meaning, but I would understand its tremendous synchronism later.

One of my favorite movies is *Groundhog Day*. In it an average weatherman, played by Bill Murray, re-lives the same day over and over again. If something bad happens, he wakes up the next morning and starts over, knowing what could happen. Now I wish for that opportunity. I want my Bella back and wish to God I could recreate that fateful day. I would do so many things differently if I could. I am willing to bargain with God.

Spiritual author/speaker Iyanla Vanzant has said that we are questioning God when we ask for things to be different. It is God's plan for things to go the way they go. It is up to us to see the gift in each experience.

I see *Groundhog Day* as a metaphor for life. Each day is a new beginning and a fresh start.

A friend sent me this passage from a Hindu philosopher:

> *Vairagya means satisfaction, the feeling that no desire is to be satisfied any more, that nothing on earth is desired. Vairagi means a person who has become indifferent; and yet indifference is not the word for it. It describes a person who has lost the value in his eyes of all that attracts the human being. It is no more attractive to him; it no more enslaves him. He may still be interested in all things of this life but is not bound to them. No affair of this world, no relation,*

*no friendship, no wealth, no rank, position or comfort, nothing holds him. And yet that does not mean that he in any way lacks what is called **love** or kindness, forever as he lives in this world it is only out of love. He is not interested in the world, it is only love that keeps him here, a love which does not express itself any more in the way of attachment; but only in the way of kindness, forgiveness, generosity, service, consideration, sympathy, helpfulness, in any way that it can; never expecting a return from the world, but ever doing all that it can. This is a great moment, and then comes that which is the kingdom of God.*

While my Bella was with me I shared kindness, love, joy, laughter. If she was meant to leave me, I must treasure those moments, be satisfied with that and not try to hang on to her. I have hung on to things, people, relationships, and experiences because of my fear of the unknown or fear of moving forward. It was easier to hold on to the familiar than to try something new. Here was another lesson.

# From Clutter to Balance

I've been preparing for a garage sale that I scheduled before I knew I might have to move. I like to declutter as often as possible. As I mentioned before, decluttering in feng shui is a major way to create movement in your life. Old things represent the past and hold you back. With Bella's passing, I am free to move forward in a new job, new place, new beginning. I had hoped to share all that with her, but it must be that my new life is meant to be focused on work and relationships.

My parents are driving in from out of town to help me. It will be the first time I have seen them since the accident. When I told them the news they were very upset. Pets definitely have an energy that can bring families closer. Bella brought out the loving side in everyone she met.

While holding on to people and pets can keep us from a full and happy life, our things can hold us back, too. I tend to be a nester. While I have moved several times since

2000, before that time I had not moved in fifteen years. While I love traveling, I like having a solid home base. My moves were all work-related and financially necessary. Each time, I de-cluttered even more.

One day at church I heard a spiritual teacher say that "we spend the first 40 years of our lives accumulating things and the last 40 getting rid of them." It seems true for me. I was in an accumulating mode when I worked in my corporate jobs. I wanted the look of success with the big house, designer décor and clothing, expensive jewelry, furnishings, and car. I had a successful husband. I had a maid. I took flying lessons and traveled all over the world…to China, Australia, Peru, Egypt, Africa, Mexico, Canada, Europe, and almost all the 50 states. But at age 42, I walked away from it all. My marriage had ended, my job was unfulfilling, and I had health issues. I wanted quality of life and some rest. I left to pursue my own business, allowing me more time for myself. One way to begin this process was to begin letting go of the things I really didn't need or love.

It has taken me six moves to de-clutter. Each time I do it, I feel better inside. I feel a weight lifted. Things have to be taken care of, managed, and stored. Less is more, as they say. I can still make a lot of money if I choose, but I don't need to keep buying things to make me happy. Making money, giving it away for good, doing what I love and being at peace are more important to me at this time in my life.

☯

I remember going to Boston one year to visit one of my brothers. On that trip I took a tour of a beautiful Victorian mansion. It had 32 rooms and every one of them was decorated beautifully. The lady who owned it was said to have lived in just one room of that big house for her whole life. I found that interesting. How much do we really need?

I remember working with a client a few years ago who was very stuck.

She wanted me to help her pick out some new furniture for her condo. While I agreed to help her, I told her I could also offer advice on the overall feng shui of the space. She was a bit hesitant but scheduled the session. Getting to the space was tricky; I had to ring the buzzer downstairs when I arrived so she could unlock the door, then I walked up the stairs to her small condo on the third floor. She was the only one on the third floor, and said the door would be open for me to walk in. It all seemed so cloak and dagger.

When I approached her door I knocked, then proceeded to walk in. I was immediately stopped by boxes stacked up at least six feet high. At 5'3", I could not see a thing. Then I heard a voice that sounded like it was coming from way back in the far corner of the space. My client called, "Come on in, pardon the boxes and the mess." I had to make my way to her through aisles created by the stacked boxes. I assumed she had just moved in, but thought I would kill any movers who left my stuff like that!

This condo was very small, at only 700 square feet. Fortunately, it had vaulted ceilings and sky lights covered the whole ceiling, allowing some Chi to flow inside. Since she was on the top floor, she could see the sky.

I walked in slowly and began to see more open space. My client was sitting in an overstuffed chair in the corner of the room. She was morbidly obese. She said she had lived in the condo for four years like this, rarely going out. The most remarkable thing was that she wanted me to help her pick out a couch and chairs that were far too large for the space. The legs on the furniture she chose were massive. I said, "Unless you need to replace something, don't waste your money. There are other, more important things to take care of right now."

I am direct with my clients. I feel it is only fair. They are paying me for my expert advice, not to tell them what they want to hear. Still, I had compassion for this client. She was definitely a candidate for the television show *Hoarders*. She had not left her space for four years, except to buy groceries. When she did leave, she had a cab pick her up downstairs, and she would pay people to deliver things to her. She was not wealthy, so this way of living was a financial drain.

I sat with her and we started talking about her things. She started to cry. She had lost her husband and it was clear that she was still grieving after many years. She felt that getting rid of things would also mean losing his memory. She was holding on to the pain of her loss. Sometimes grief can also be a way of hiding from life. If you are afraid to move forward, you can always tell yourself it is because you are still grieving.

While it is natural for sadness to come and go after someone has passed, we don't want to hang on to those feelings in a way that makes us unhappy. We want to be aware of the feelings and let them move through us, remembering our loved ones happily and with gratitude for the time we were able to share with them. I helped this client see that, by releasing some of her things, she would find more energy, better health, and less depression. She'd had those skylights installed so she would have some light coming in, but they were causing too much loss of Chi, instead of creating the balance she needed. At the end of our session, she agreed to get rid of stacks of newspapers and magazines that were ten years old. She agreed not to buy any new furniture for a while. It would be a day-by-day process, but one that would eventually transform her life. I recommended a professional organizer, and after a few months I checked in to see how she was doing. She was more organized, had a lighter space, and had even begun walking for exercise and losing some weight.

This client was an extreme example of how stuffing your feelings can create weight gain and many other problems. In feng shui, if you just de-clutter, you can lose weight if you choose. Clutter offers a false sense of protection and safety. With lots of things surrounding you, you feel less vulnerable. Clutter in the home is like extra weight on the body. As spiritual author and teacher Louise Hay writes, carrying extra fat falsely satisfies the need for protection.

In today's busy world, our homes play an important part in helping us recharge our batteries. In feng shui, the home represents our inner world and a mirror reflection of our current life. We cannot control the chaos of the outside world, so it is important we create beauty and flow inside, no matter how small or modest a form it might take. This way we can take this harmonious feeling with us wherever we go.

I love a Taoist quote that says:

> *If there is peace in the heart, there is peace in the home, if there is peace in the home, there is peace in the community, if there is peace in the community, there is peace in the world.*

# Telling Children about Death

Today is the day I usually see the little girl I mentor through the Big Sister program. I go once a week to her school at lunchtime, and have often brought Bella with me. We would play on the playground and do craft projects or read books. I don't have the heart to tell her that Bella has passed away. She's only nine and I am not sure how she will take it.

Mary is a nine-year-old Hispanic girl, the eldest of five children. She takes care of her four younger siblings when she gets home from school. Mary's parents have very little in the way of money, so they aren't able to give Mary dolls, clothes, etc. When I visit with her, we make jewelry that she likes to give as gifts to her mom, grandmother, or friends at school. She is quite creative. My role as her Big Sister is to be a mentor. We talk during our visits. My intention is to build trust, so that she feels comfortable enough with me to share if she ever has a problem or is in any danger.

For extra fun, I would often take Bella on my visits to see Mary. The first few times, the kids on the playground swarmed us like bees. They all wanted to pet Bella and would have their hands all over her. Once they chased her all around the playground, which really scared her. Since that time, Mary and I would find our own quiet place for our personal time instead. Because the area where we would sit was fenced in, I would let Bella run around without a leash with joy for a few minutes. Mary loved playing with Bella and letting her jump on her lap to lick her face.

I went to the school to tell Mary about Bella's passing today. The day started out with cold temperatures, but by noon the sun was shining brightly. I brought Mary some lunch so we could eat together outside on the school picnic tables. The first thing she asked was if Bella was with me. I told her no and that we had a problem, promising to share it with her when we sat down for lunch. I wore dark sunglasses to hide my tears. I was sort of hoping she would forget about it, but as soon as we started walking, she asked about the problem I had with Bella.

I told Mary that Bella had been with me while I was running an errand. A loud noise bothered her, she ran into the street, and she was hit by a car. The first words out of Mary's mouth were, "¿Ella murio?" In Spanish this phrase means *She died?* I said yes, she died.

As we walked, I further explained what had happened. I told her that I hadn't been to see her the week before because I had been too sad. Such a little adult, Mary said, "Pobrecita, era tan bonita," which means, *Poor little thing, she was so pretty.* With my sunglasses still on, I started to cry. Mary didn't cry, but I heard her sniffling. I think she kept some tears inside. She mentioned that she'd had a pet that had died when she lived in Mexico. She and her family came to the U.S. when she was a baby.

The next day was Valentine's Day, so we sat down to make cards for her schoolmates. We talked about Bella and the afternoon turned out to be one of sharing and fun. Children are much stronger than we think. To this day, Mary still mentions the time she spent with Bella, and remembers it fondly.

Working at that children's hospital when I first got out of college, I remember the tiny children telling their parents not to cry. They had no sense of death, only life and being in the moment. They handle grief as well as you do. When I told Mary about Bella and showed some tears, it allowed her to express her feelings. We talked about Bella and shared some time together. I didn't hide the news from her, or tell her the story in a way that wasn't true.

A lesson I've taken from this is that what we focus on is what we get in our lives. Focus on pain and sadness, and you will get more of it. While the children I saw in hospital beds might have felt bad, they cheered up anytime you came to visit. Their energy changed when an adult came in looking sad.

A friend sent me this story about a week ago and I saved it. It reveals to me the reason I was to wait to get this book out. It is so touching; it makes me cry to read it.

*Our 14-year-old dog Abbey passed away last month. Our 4-year-old daughter Meredith was crying and talking about how much she missed Abbey and if she could write a letter to God so when Abbey got to heaven, God would recognize her. I told her we could do so and she dictated these words:*

Dear God:

Would you please take care of my dog? She died yesterday and is with you in heaven. I miss her so much. I know you let me have her even when she was sick. I hope you will play with her. She likes to swim and play with balls. I am sending you a picture of her so you will know she really is my dog. I really miss her.

Love,

Meredith

*We put the letter in an envelope with a picture of Abbey and Meredith and addressed it to God/Heaven. We put our return address on it. We added lots of stamps as Abbey said it would take several to get all the way to heaven. That afternoon Abbey dropped it in the letter box at the post office. A few days later Abbey asked if God had gotten the letter yet. I told her I thought he had. Yesterday there was a package in gold wrapping addressed to "Meredith" in unfamiliar handwriting. She opened it and inside was a book by Mr. Rogers called "When a Pet Dies." Taped to the inside was the original letter we wrote to God in its opened envelope. On the opposite page was a picture of Abbey and Meredith with this note:*

Dear Meredith:

Abbey arrived safely in heaven and I recognized her right away. Abbey isn't sick anymore and her spirit is here with me just like it stays in your heart. Abbey loved being your dog and since we don't need our bodies in heaven, I don't have any pockets to keep your picture in so I am sending it back to you in this little book for you to have something to keep and remember Abbey by.

Thank you for the beautiful letter and thank your mother for helping you write it and sending it to me. What a wonderful mother you have. I picked her for you. I send my blessings every day and know that I love you very much. By the way, I am easy to find. I am wherever there is love.

Love, God

How beautiful! From Abbey the dog, who brought so much love to Meredith and the family, to Meredith who loved Abbey so much, to her mom who loved Abbey and Meredith and let her write the letter, and finally, to the compassionate postman who wrote back.

If we look at how much joy and love our pets have brought us we can slowly feel better about them being gone. Their spirit is always with us in our hearts.

# They Don't Go Anywhere

L ast night was the night of Bella's death. I've heard some say that they could still feel their pet's spirit in the house after they've died. I know what they mean. You feel their energy.

Bella used to sleep with me. She would lie on a pillow next to me; her whole body only took up the middle of the pillow. Before she fell asleep, she would often settle in somewhere near my feet. She was hot-natured but if it was cold outside, she would shiver. She felt like a hot potato lying next to me, which was great during cold winter nights. Eventually we would both find our comfortable spots on the bed, always close to each other. Last night I felt warmth and a heaviness near my feet, like something was there. Was I imagining it? Or was it really her?

I had read my cards earlier. I have used the ancient tarot deck to help me receive messages from spirit many times before. Having used them for so many years, I feel they speak to me now. There is no magic here; it is really my higher self speaking to me. But seeing things visually on a card helps jog my memory and helps me understand the messages that come. It is like when something you read in the newspaper reminds you of someone and just after that, they call. Some call it intuition, some may say it is a form of clairvoyance, but I find that the information is always within you.

Everything is connected. In laying out the cards I asked if Bella had passed on to another life yet. The answer was that she had not. She missed me as much as I missed her, but she was ready to move on. After reading the cards I spoke out loud to her. I told her that I missed her and loved her very much and wanted her here with me to share in everything. I understood that was not to be. The Universe had a bigger plan for us both. I wished her joy and love in her new journey. I wanted her to know she could visit me anytime and that she would always be with me in my heart. We would never be apart and, no matter how busy she was in her new life, she could visit me anytime. I would welcome it.

I fell asleep. Around 4:00 am I was in a dead sleep, but woke when I felt something run across my bed. It had so much energy and vitality it woke me up. It felt like a small dog running back and forth on the bed. I jumped up wondering, "What the heck was that?" It felt so real. Bella was light and did not have that kind of weight or strength. I have heard that when a soul passes, it is more vital and stronger than when it was alive. Could that have been Bella full grown, energetic, and healthy, coming back for a visit to let me know she was okay and happy? I definitely believe so. I felt her energy so strongly.

The next morning, I received an email from a friend with this prayer. I am grateful that blessings and signals come in many ways. I am open to them all.

> *For everyone who asks receives; he who seeks finds; and to him who knocks, the door will be opened.* (Matthew 7:8).

Is there something you have been asking for from God or the Universe? Does it seem like it's taking a long time to come to pass? Be encouraged today! Through faith and patience you will inherit the promise. You can trust that the Spirit's word is true. Submit your prayers and keep an attitude of faith and expectancy. Keep asking. Keep seeking. Keep knocking on the door, and it will open for you. It may seem to take a long time, but know this: The Universe is working behind the scenes on your behalf. It is orchestrating things in your favor. It is perfecting whatever concerns you. Don't give up! Start thanking Spirit for its faithfulness in your life. As you stay faithful in your prayers and gratitude, the Universe will move mightily on your behalf. It will take you places you've never dreamed of, and you will live the life of victory it has in store for you!

But be careful what you ask for. I asked my angels to help me find my Bella on that fateful day, and they did. I was not meant to have her with me in the physical form anymore, but they let me find her so I could see her and bring her home. Now I pray for her healing and mine, and trust that there is a higher purpose in it all. I also know that she was always with me and a part of me, and that she is really still here.

# Going Within

*I*t has been a week since Bella's death. I decided to go to my yoga class tonight. It's the first time since the accident that I have allowed myself to go within. I have prayed, walked, and been quiet, but not really silent.

At the end of each class, the teacher leads us in a light meditation so we can let go of any feelings that might be blocking our channels of joy. The music he plays while speaking is so soft, calming, and spiritual. While I lay on my mat, my eyes started welling up with tears. They just began flowing. All the memories of the past week, Bella's happy face, energy, and love, were right in front of me in vivid color. The yoga room was pretty dark but I guess the teacher could tell I was crying. I was tearful but quiet. As he continued the meditation, he sat next to me and held my hand. My eyes were closed, but during the entire meditation I felt his comforting gesture.

When it was over, I got up and thanked him. He said he could feel that I was in pain. He had met Bella, and he and his wife had even babysat her. They were the only ones besides my parents who'd had this privilege. She had been so young, and I'd been uncomfortable leaving her with people. The instructor and his wife were a warm couple without children or pets. They had met Bella and really liked her. I had taken them up on their offer to watch her while I attended a meditation retreat. They'd enjoyed playing with her and taking her for walks, so they were upset to hear my news.

One of the main things I continue to do in my life is be grateful. It is a natural law that gratitude leads to abundance in every way. I am so grateful for my kind friends and family. I have seen sides to people I had not seen before. Many were touched by Bella, her death, and my grief.

Gratitude also keeps us out of depression and focusing on the sad things. When we are grateful each day we can appreciate the wonderful moments we did have with our loved ones who are no longer with us.

Today is Valentine's Day. I did not go to the fundraiser. Still, I will help the winning pet owner set up a feng shui space for their dog. Dogs feel energy and need a space that is theirs, even if they occasionally sleep with you. From puppyhood to her grand old age of eight months, Bella had her own little feng shui den. It wasn't a crate, but a tent with her toys and some towels and blankets for her to sleep in. I kept it near the back patio door so she could look outside and see the birds and squirrels. When we would come home from a long day, she would immediately roll around in it and lay down. When I was out, I would leave soft music playing for her. When I came home, she might lie on my lap while I watched TV or sit in my chair while I made dinner. She would go to her tent when she didn't want me to bother her. She didn't like baths, so at bath time she would hide there.

I felt sad that Bella was not with me to go to the fundraising event. I was not up for socializing so I ordered a pizza and rented *Chocolat*, starring Johnny Depp and Juliette Binoche. I felt lonely, missed Bella, and needed a feel-good movie. I don't think I was the only one doing this on Valentine's Day.

I loved how creative Juliette Binoche's character was, and the free-spiritedness of Johnny Depp's character. In the movie Juliette's character feng shui-ed her candy shop by placing red cures over her doors for protection, which was fun to watch. She had so much zest for life and exuded much passion to make her candy store work, even against all odds. I could relate. It also kept my mind off of my sadness for a few hours.

# It's Okay to Be Angry

Today I am angry with Bella. It's the first time I have felt this way.

According to Dr. Elizabeth Kubler-Ross' book *On Death and Dying*, we go through stages in our grief. As a social worker back in the 80s, this book helped me work with families who had children with terminal illnesses. One of the best books written about dealing with death and dying, it was and still is a profound book. One of its theories is that people go through stages in their grief process; if one of the stages is missed, full healing cannot occur. People can go through the stages in different orders, stay in one stage forever, or go back and forth from one to another. The first stage is Denial, then Anger, Bargaining, Depression, and Acceptance. I have found this to be true in my work as a social worker, and in my own recent experience.

In my mind I've been asking Bella why she ran away from me on that day. Why did she keep running when I called for her? I am angry with her for leaving me. I know this is not fair but it is how I feel. I am angry at myself for not protecting her.

I had given up on staying in the house where we spent our time together. It was being sold and I was going to have to move. But now I decided to fight for it. I talked to a mortgage lender to see if I qualified to buy it. He called me back to tell me I had been approved for the loan. Now that I had the opportunity to buy the house, it made me sad. My housing situation would be settled, but Bella would not be there to share it.

Bella loved the backyard. Whenever I went to the patio door, she would run and jump until I opened it. She would dash out with large leaps. She was determined to get one of those squirrels. She would whimper and almost squeal until I opened the door for her to do her chasing. It was if the squirrels were playing with her. They would stay low to the ground until she came out running, then they would scurry up the tree but only halfway, just to where she could not reach. They would circle the tree trunk, going up and down, up and down – making her go crazy. She loved it! After the squirrels went away and the excitement died down she would patrol the yard, taking it all in. She owned it. It was her turf and she knew it.

We also had a possum under the house. Bella always kept her eye out for him. She would go under the house, where he had dug a large hole to come in and out. Every time I opened the patio door, she went there first. I would call in a loud voice, "Don't go there!" and she would turn around. She did it every time, though, so she must have just wanted to see if I was alert… or hoped that one time I might not be watching!

Now that I am buying this house I will be able to fix it up and landscape the yard in a way that would have been wonderful for her. But now, the house just doesn't feel the same without her. She brought life to it.

Pets do that. They are considered good feng shui. They bring in Chi. Bella ran all around the house and every bit of it has her energy. This is one of the reasons I felt so sad when I came home after losing her.

Bella had to explore everything. Although I watched her diligently, when she was a baby she chewed everything she could get her teeth on. I had plenty of chew toys around, but she loved cords. She managed to chew the cords to my stereo speaker, my computer speakers, and my cellphone headset. (I got a new headset but the others I have managed to do without.) Puppies like to chew. You can't get mad at them for that any more than you can scold a baby for teething. Get them plenty of exercise and keep lots of chew toys on hand and you'll be in good shape.

Whenever I couldn't take Bella out, I would throw the ball for her to chase. We would play that game until she wore out. She loved to play tug of war with her toys, too, and for me to chase her. When she got older, I would sometimes take her to the park when no one was around, then let her off her leash and start chasing her. She and I would get a heavy dose of exercise.

Keeping your dog exercised will burn off some of that energy or frustration they have built up from being inside all day. It tears me up to hear of people putting their dogs in crates all day, sometimes up to ten hours, so they don't destroy the house. A dog can be trained not to mess up your home! Get a session with a good dog trainer. Get a doggie door, gate off a room, or just plain don't get a dog if you don't have time to walk it or let it roam free in the house or yard. It's just plain cruel. It's not surprising that some of these pets develop emotional or potty training issues.

Missing Bella a lot today. I put a contract on the house I am living in. If I get it, it will be my home, along with all its memories of Bella. Why couldn't she be here to share all this with me?

It's a rainy Saturday, and I cried as I drove around today, glancing back to the back seat where Bella would have been.

I'm depressed. It is time to change my thoughts. I have read and studied many philosophies on how our thoughts create our reality. We can control our own thoughts. This was sent to me recently, which I found useful regarding this issue.

## Undistracted Energy
*from Pure Thoughts*

> *Our thoughts usually scatter in a vast array of directions. They start and stop and move in surprising ways from one second to the next. If we try to follow our thoughts without controlling them, we will be amazed at how truly inconsistent they are. Yet, if we apply our minds to a specific task, especially one that interests us, they gather together and allow us to focus our attention, creating great power and energy. This is what is known as pure thought, because it is undistracted.*

> *We can simply respond to the opportunities that naturally come our way. When this is the essence of our experience, we can go with the flow, knowing that we will be okay.*

I did this in my relationship with Bella. I was enjoying the moments with her. Maybe I was too focused on her. She was my distraction. I did what I enjoyed. I worked with clients, didn't go to networking groups I didn't like, followed up on leads, and just plain had fun with her. We would go to parks during the week during my lunchtime.

I did work-related activities, but mostly enjoyed being in the moment with her. She taught me that skill.

The day she died, I was not as focused on her. I was worried about my living situation. I was distracted. Did that cause her to leave my vibrational field? Had she been my sole focus that day, would she still be with me? My feeling is that she might still be here.

Someone sent this to me. I read it to feel better.

## Live with Joy

*Find joy in doing nothing and you can find it in everything.*

*Imagine living this day filled with joy, happiness and positive purpose.*

*Let go of any concern you may have for what does or does not come your way.*

*Focus instead on the good and valuable things that you can give, create, inspire and choose to experience.*

**Bella was not just my dog, she was my friend. I was sent this comforting poem…**

*Pets come into our lives for a reason, a season or a lifetime.*

*When you know which one it is, you will know what to do for them.*

*When a furry friend is in your life for a REASON, it is usually to meet a need you have expressed.*

*It is said that love is blind but friendship is clairvoyant …..*

*Author Unknown*

I looked up this poem and there are several versions of it with author unknown. I love it because it says so beautifully to me that my Bella's time on Earth is done, and my work with her is also done. It is okay for her to move on and for me to be happy again.

One week after Bella's passing, I went back to the Humane Society's pet loss group. As I was driving there, I got lost. I could not find it with any directions I had. It ended up being only five minutes from my house. I saw many cars there and that scared me. I didn't want a big group. I was still too fragile inside. When I arrived I was directed to a small room in the back where the door was ajar. I was 15 minutes late and the group was already in session.

There were only two people and a facilitator. One woman lost her dog to cancer a few years back, and another was losing her dog to cancer. Both were distraught. I wondered why I had come. I really didn't want to hear about those things. But I sat down and listened.

Both pets were older dogs. My Bella was only 8 months. How I wished that I'd had had that many years with her! Losing a pet to an illness like cancer is something you can't help. Losing a dog because she was not on a leash was my fault. I was still feeling that guilt. The facilitator asked me if I had a dog that was ill or had passed. I said I had lost my little Bella a week earlier after she was hit by a car. I had managed to keep my thoughts on the other people so I would not cry, but when she asked the question tears flowed down my face.

I said that I had always been regarded by others and myself as highly responsible, and I felt like a failure because I didn't protect something I loved so dearly. The therapist was comforting. She said there was no way I could have predicted Bella's reaction. It would have been just as easy for her to have crossed the street and waited there, or not crossed the street at all and just run around the corner until I caught up with her. The therapist's words made sense. I then opened up my heart and began listening to the other ladies' stories. It was apparent that, no matter what age, the bond you have with your pet is so unique and strong it is painful to lose them. And every person's way of grieving is different.

My parents visited a few weeks later. They came to help

with my garage sale. I also think they came to see how I was doing and to offer support. I needed that from them. We spent a beautiful sunny day out in the front yard.

While we were running an errand together, my brother made an interesting observation. He noticed my spiritual CDs in the car and commented on how long I had been listening to them. He thought they were old but they were actually the newer versions of the Tao and the Law of Attraction. He said, "I get what these people are saying, but what I don't understand is why things happen like what happened to Bella." I told him I had asked the same questions. Even though I have studied many of the scriptures, Hindu philosophy, Taoist, Buddhist teachings, and more, my pain was so great I could not seek solace in them. Now, a few weeks later, things were beginning to make some sense to me. These things don't always have to make sense, but understanding on some level why things happen can bring some inner peace.

One of my favorite movies even though I could not watch until some time had passed, is Hachi, with Richard Gere. It is an emotional, heart-warming movie. It is based on a true story of a faithful Akita puppy who falls into the lap of a man that lands up adopting him. Each time the man goes to work and rides the train the dog follows him and waits until he comes home. One day the man dies. The dog continues to go to the train station to wait for him for over ten years in rain, snow, cold, and heat. Hachi finally dies at the same spot where he waited for his owner all those years. His soul is then reunited with the spirit of his master and he is smiling again. The love and devotion pets have for us is like no other. This is a must see movie.

I truly believe that our furry friends have souls. Souls have a path. My Bella's path here ended. She was on the path to her next life and nothing I could do was going to stop her from going.

One of the many things I have realized is how lonely I have been. I longed for affection and companionship more than I knew. With Bella my heart opened up. I felt lighter, happier, and more at peace.

When people say their blood pressure dropped to normal rates after adopting a pet, I understand why. Love is the strongest energy and a powerful healer. Coming home to a pet that's excited to see you and happy to be with you at any time of the day is something wonderful.

I saw a t-shirt once that said, "Don't medicate, meditate." I'd like one that says, "Don't fret, get a pet." Pets take your mind off of yourself in the same way that giving to others does. You don't have time to feel sad, lonely, or angry when your pet is happily waiting for you to play with them or take them for a walk. They will wait for you forever. It is why we must treasure our moments with them.

# Compartmentalizing Grief

It is three weeks since Bella's passing and I finally went to my meditation group tonight. It has been tough to sit quietly or listen to songs about love. I've been concentrating on managing my daily tasks and work projects, keeping my grief on the back burner until I had time to go there. It hasn't been easy and sometimes the tears have come at unexpected times.

At the end of our meditation evening, a very nice woman in the group with a comforting energy asked how I was doing. She said she thinks about me all the time, because she knows how it feels to have lost a pet. I told her I have many reminders; I walk into my home and Bella's pictures and things are everywhere. She commented that it must be hard seeing her things, assuming that it would bring up the pain all over again. I had not thought of it that way.

The first few weeks I needed to keep everything of Bella's near me. I needed to feel her energy. Now it has become real that she is not coming back, and seeing her things has started to make me miss her even more. So, tonight I packed her crate and all of her toys, food bowls, etc., away in a closet. I'll keep them there to use again when I am ready for a new pet, but I no longer need to see them when I first walk in the door.

I have framed pictures of Bella everywhere. It is time to put some of them away. Her ashes and picture are in my bedroom. I may move them soon, but am not ready yet to bury her. I also made a beautiful photo album, where I keep a letter I wrote wishing her a safe and happy passing. I made a CD presentation of her life that I sent out to close friends as a memorial. I've also been wearing the dog tags that she had on the day she died. I will put these in a special place. I miss her and wish she was still here, but reliving the pain of her death is not healthy or helping me move on. It is also not good feng shui.

My meditation group's annual silent retreat is next week. Although I was scheduled to go and paid in full, I was not going to go. I didn't want to be crying the whole time. In past weeks I've been spending much of my time alone. At the retreat, while silent, I will be with many people and privacy may not be available. Still, the retreat is about cultivating inner peace, being mindful of our actions, and living in the present moment. I need to go.

If I still had Bella, I might not have gone. Who would I have left her with for the weekend? What if something had happened to her while I was gone? I would never have forgiven myself. I see so many people with dogs that are not cared for like Bella. Some owners keep their dogs locked up most of the day, hardly ever play with them, and yet somehow the dogs survive. I took Bella everywhere and we walked daily. She might have been more at risk that way, but life is a risk. We might avoid accidents by never going out but that is no way to live, nor is it fair to the pet.

I spent a lot of time on the Internet, reading, and talking to people about Yorkshire Terriers before I got Bella. I wanted to be prepared and be a good owner. Now I know that, with my experience and knowledge, I will be much better next time. I will always, always keep my pets on leash unless I know for sure that we are totally alone in an environment that is safe for dogs their size. I will have my dogs professionally trained to understand what it means to **stop** and to **come**. Unfortunately I had to learn these lessons the hard way, but I look forward to the day I can bring another baby home and give it a good life.

As I said before, I can never replace Bellaluna, but I have started to look forward to a new and worthwhile experience in the near future with another pet.

# The Retreat

*J* 've never had any deaths in my immediate family or lost someone close, so this was my first experience with real loss. I feel the Universe is preparing me to be strong.

Once you enter your fifties, things start to change dramatically. You become more introspective, slow down, and start wanting to simplify your life. You learn to treasure your moments. You take less negativity from people, yet become more accepting. I feel everything so much more, maybe because when I was young I stayed so busy striving and accumulating to feel worthy that I didn't have time to stop and smell the roses. This is a time to not be afraid of transition, change, or death, but to embrace them.

Love deeply with all your heart and if that love leaves, love again. The Buddha said, "Life is about impermanence." Knowing that is one thing, but experiencing it can be frightening – especially when we don't want to let go of something so special to us. We must understand that we really don't own anything. We cannot control life's destiny.

It is our job to go with the flow of life, the Tao, in the most harmonious way possible. Your flow is not my flow. Your path is yours and mine is mine. Understanding this has made me much more accepting of other people who might push my buttons. They are reacting the way they do because it is their destiny to do so. They have lessons to learn as well.

I was sent this beautiful quote from a book by W. Bruce Cameron…

"Dogs come into our lives to teach us about love, they depart to teach us about loss. A new dog never replaces an old dog; it merely expands the heart. If you have loved many dogs your heart is very big".

**All is Well**
**Death is nothing at all**
**I have only slipped into the next room**
**I am I and you are you…..**

*Canon Henry Scott Holland*

Well, I went to my meditation retreat after all, thanks to some insistence from friends. I did fine most of the time, with a few tears now and then. We had an afternoon to visit with our Zen master teacher and ask him anything we want. He offers his time and insights so generously. People who want to can sign up for a 15-minute session with him during one of our three days.

The retreat is nestled in the beauty of a nature park just a few miles outside of Austin, Texas. We eat, meditate, walk, brush our teeth, etc., in silence. It is a powerful experience. When I first heard about it I thought I could only handle a day of silence at the most, but once I attended, I quickly realized that you need the extra days to really settle into the experience.

We come in with monkey brains from the busy worlds we live in. Chatter is constantly going on in our heads, so to slow our minds down is a skill that takes practice and time. Anyone can do it, though, and people from all over the country of different religious affiliations attend the retreat to practice the art. I usually come away feeling more centered, grounded, and peaceful. The effects last for a long time.

I was afraid to ask a question of our teacher; I was worried that I would cry in front of him and be embarrassed. I was still grieving. I noticed that, whenever someone at the retreat asked me how I was doing and I mentioned the passing of my pet, they cut the conversation short. It was too much for them to handle. I understood. Better to wait and speak to the teacher anyway.

I'd had lunch and was feeling pretty grounded when my turn came around. It was a beautiful sunny day in March and he was sitting outside at a picnic bench under a canopy of trees. I slowly walked up to his table and bowed, giving him a timid smile. Bowing to our teacher or anyone in the group is honoring the Buddha nature (compassionate and loving) within us all.

Our teacher, a quiet and gentle man, sat awaiting my question. I took a deep breath and told him I had just lost my dear pet. With a trembling voice I said, "I am so sad. I just don't know how I will get over this. What is my lesson here?" Calmly and without missing a beat, he answered, "Impermanence. She came to teach you impermanence, as well as love and joy and all the other things you felt about her. Nothing in life stays forever. That is why we must treasure the moments." I sat with those words for a few moments.

Then this brought on the waterworks. He said, "You know, she was a pet. She wasn't a rock. You loved her. She showed you how capable you are of really loving and the kind of compassion you possess. You wouldn't be sad or in such pain if you didn't care deeply about her."

Wow. How heartfelt, meaningful, and comforting that session was for me. For this I have been grateful to my teacher, my sangha (group, community), and my mindfulness practice.

# Forgiveness

With these new insights I realized that, for me to have real closure, I needed to forgive.

I needed to forgive the FedEx guy for slamming the door to his truck, which caused Bella to bolt off running to her death. I had to see him as a person who might have been having a really bad day. He might have had some bad news or a sick child, been going through a divorce, you name it.

Did I mention that my former husband worked for FedEx? Here is the synchronicity of life playing out again to reveal its connections. I find this so revealing and fascinating. Perhaps some final forgiveness work was needed on my part to heal that past relationship. Was I still holding on to past resentments? I didn't think so, as my divorce was years ago. Was the slamming of the FedEx truck's door symbolic in closing that chapter of my life for good?

It seems that change was in the air in many ways, with a new year, the loss of Bella, and my releasing of negative emotions.

I needed to forgive the woman who had called me on my cellphone, distracting me so that I was not quick in responding when Bella jumped out of my bag. It could have been anyone calling.

I needed to forgive the people in my life whom I'd considered close friends but had been insensitive during my time of grief. Not being there for me during that time doesn't make them bad people.

Above all, I needed to forgive myself. I blamed myself for Bella's death. I could not shake this feeling. It wasn't until the retreat that I finally came to accept her death and all that it meant.

Acceptance does not mean agreeing with or condoning a situation, but rather seeing the reality of what is. Once I accepted that Bella was truly gone, I could see more clearly to forgive myself. I've read that much of alcoholism is unresolved grief. I am sure this is the same for drugs or any addiction. What have you not forgiven yourself or others for in your life? What losses, regrets, or failed dreams have you experienced but not yet mourned? Suppressing those feelings with alcohol or drugs keeps you stuck and can eventually kill you. It halts the flow of life. Being gentle and compassionate with ourselves is one of the keys to happiness.

# Closure

C losure can be found in many ways. It is different for everyone, but must happen in order for life to continue. I don't see closure as shutting the door and never looking back, but rather as releasing. Once we find closure we can allow ourselves to let go and appreciate all that a lost loved one offered us. We can find some peace, comfort, and even joy in remembering them for all they were.

Seeing Bella at the vet's office when she died, the altar I created, the photo album of her life, the online memorial I sent to my friends and the goodbye letter I wrote her… these were all tools I used to heal my grief. One chapter must close for another to open, however painful it might be in the beginning. This is the Tao.

One of the members of my meditation group sent this quote via e-mail which helped to set things right in my mind about letting go

## Regret Not Guilt

*"The difference between regret and guilt is that the guilt never faces the wrongdoing straightforwardly. There is just this strong emotion of 'I wish I hadn't done it, I wish it hadn't happened, I wish I hadn't gotten angry, I wish I hadn't said that embarrassing thing,' and so on...*

*Regret is the opposite of guilt. We acknowledge it, we expose to ourselves that we have done something harmful and how it came about from our ignorance, but we don't get caught up in emotions or story lines."*

Let us not regret what has happened but instead value the time we did have with our loved ones, knowing that if we had not cared deeply we would not be suffering. It shows our capacity to love. This was my lesson.

# A New Beginning

After three long months since Bella's passing, I have decided to add to my family again. Had you asked me when she died if I could do this, I would have said a flat NO. I couldn't imagine it.

But… pets are considered good feng shui so it's no wonder we love them. I remember my trip to China in 1996 for my training in Classical Feng Shui. We visited the Emperor's palaces, since they employed feng shui masters. The masters insisted that deer with big antlers must be present on the properties, because they were considered good luck. The animals wandered around the premises.

Pets bring in Chi. If they are healthy and happy, they add to your good feng shui. It is said that, when buying a property or new house, you should look at the vegetation and the animals around the neighborhood. Are the plants and trees flourishing? Do the pets appear to be in good health? If so, the area has good Chi.

As I said, I couldn't imagine having a new pet ever again. I was so sad after Bella's passing; I also felt it would be dishonoring her in some way. It felt too soon. But, since love is what really counts, I decided that giving love to another animal in need would be the right thing to do. I knew it would help me heal and bring good energy into my home. So I decided to adopt again.

I knew I wanted another female Yorkshire Terrier so she could wear all of Bella's beautiful clothes. (I later realized that buying all new clothes for the new pup would have been a better option. My new Yorkie was not Bella, and wearing her clothes might prolong my sadness.) I looked at the Yorkie rescue sites and even places where people were selling pups up to a year old, but nothing was available. I finally decided on a puppy after I saw an ad in the Sunday paper.

I went to see the puppies knowing full well I would not be able to come home without one. I knew I was rescuing this little puppy because she was in an unsanitary place where puppies of all kinds were being bred. I met with the owner, picked out my pup, and made arrangements to pick her up in a couple of weeks. I knew I would make another trip just to check on her.

On my follow-up trip, another little puppy ran alongside her, following as she made her way to me. I had always regretted Bella being an only pet because she was on her own when I had to go out. A playmate would have been so great for her. I asked the breeder about getting both the boy and girl. She gave me a great price, so I couldn't refuse. I also felt good about rescuing another puppy from that place.

When I went back a few weeks later to pick them up and get their papers, the breeder brought out the two puppies. They were so incredibly adorable. As I held them both, they fell asleep in my lap. I asked the breeder, "Which one is the girl?" She lifted them both up to check. She said they were both boys. I said, "What?" I specifically came for a girl; the little boy was an afterthought. She even had all the paperwork filled out with boy and girl. She apologized profusely and said she had sold the girl but had another litter and I could pick out the girl from there. She would not be ready, though, for another two weeks. I might have just walked away then, since this lady was so disorganized, but I felt those puppies needed good homes. So I went to pick out the female and took the male home.

In retrospect, it was good that I had one of them for two weeks alone. It allowed me to start some potty training and bonding before bringing the other one home. When I went to pick up the female two weeks later, she had changed dramatically. She was even more beautiful with a dark, thick, lustrous coat and a teddy bear face.

I named her Gracie Bell. Grace is a name I have always loved; it reminds me of the Grace of God, which has been such a prevalent energy in my life. Bell was in honor of Bella. I named my boy Bodhi, short for Bodhisattva, meaning angel or messenger in Buddhist philosophy. Both names honor my spiritual traditions, Catholicism and Buddhism. I call them my little Zen masters, as they teach me so much about being in the moment and having patience.

They have been loads of fun. They play, tumble, chase, and just plain love being together. They have a tight bond. If I take one on an errand for some alone time with Mom, they jump on each other with joy when they see each other again. People often wonder if two are more work. I wondered this as well, but have found that it works better. It helps with training; when one isn't catching on and the other is, they learn from one another. They also comfort each other and get plenty of exercise playing together.

I chose to have them spayed and neutered, because I didn't want more puppies. I really wanted them to have companionship. Bodhi looks like Bella and reminds me of her with some of the different facial expressions he makes. They are both great pets who are lovable and make me laugh. I hug them daily, remembering how I used to do that with Bella. This helps in the healing. I read that hugging is good for the heart, so we all benefit. The memories of Bella haven't gone away, but they have moved to a place in my heart that I can go to whenever I choose.

# Honor Your Loved One

For me, part of the forgiveness process involved nurturing myself and doing something to honor Bella's memory. I began a local meetup of Yorkshire Terrier owners in 2008; we get together monthly for our Yorkies to play together. It gives our pets an opportunity to socialize. It is easy for pets to be surrounded by humans all day, but they also need to be comfortable with other dogs so there is not fear or anxiety when in their presence.

I enjoy our gatherings because I love seeing my pets have such a good time. I also get to visit with other owners. I have had the opportunity to provide some comfort and resources to members in our group who have lost their pets. It is great to see owners socialize with one another about pet issues and their personal lives. We even help Yorkies in need find forever homes when we can. We are not a rescue group, but we are a resource.

I still have not buried her ashes. I do mostly container gardening and have a place in my backyard where I keep a live beautiful plant or flower pot. I keep her ashes there, in a container that I can later take with me if I move. I hope to find the right place for them soon. I know Bella's spirit is not in those ashes, but I still want a special place for them.

In feng shui it is not good to keep ashes of the deceased in the home. It represents energy that is yin, or low. It does not lift or enhance the flow of Chi; if wanting to improve some area of your life, you need something active. It is better to create a beautiful area that looks more like a garden than a cemetery, if you decide to bury your pet in the backyard. This way, when you see it you are reminded of your pet in a beautiful way. The flowers that grow there represent growth and the cycle of life. In feng shui, flowers are good luck.

My feng shui practice is based on a Taoist philosophy. It has helped me get through a difficult time in my life. Its principle of going with the flow of life was at the core of my healing. I needed balance restored then, and in so many other times of my life. When I left my corporate job, got a divorce, was mugged, etc., I needed balance back in my life.

I am so fortunate to have had a photo session with Bella just a couple of months before she died. They really captured her personality… so alive, happy, and playful. I'm so glad I have those mementos. I treasure the moments I have with my new pups enjoying my time with them, and I take lots of pictures because I know that they, too, will be gone someday. Being more aware and living in the present moment is my spiritual practice. This is the message of the Tao, and living a life with good feng shui.

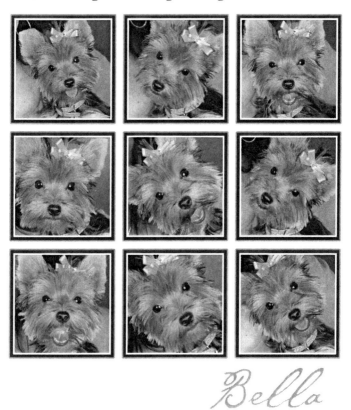

Bella

# Rescues

$\mathcal{J}$f you feel inclined, consider becoming a parent to a new pet from a rescue organization. I have heard some people say they don't own pets or would not get another because it is too painful to lose them, but if you take the focus off of yourself and realize how many unwanted pets are waiting to find a caring person and home, you may change your mind. In the U.S. alone over 4 million dogs are euthanized each year. Help this problem. Spay and Neuter your pets. Adopt from a local shelter.

There are many beautiful animals who are in great health, but just don't have forever homes. If you adopt one you will be both giving love and getting love, and that is very healing for all. You will be rescuing yourself, in a way.

One book I read after Bella died was about an attorney who lost his dog of many years, which had also been his best friend. After his precious pet passed he rescued another, which eventually died, then another. I was inspired by this. Yes, he was helping a poor defenseless animal each time but more importantly, he was expanding his heart. It takes a person of great compassion to do this kind act. What a world it could be, if we all thought this way!

I saw this message with a beautiful photo of a golden retreiver that I had to share.

"Before humans die, they write their last Will and Testament, give their home and all they have, to those they leave behind. If, with my paws, I could do the same, this is what I'd ask…

To a poor and lonely stray I'd give:

-the hand that stroked my fur and the sweet voice which spoke my name.

I'd Will to the sad, scared shelter dog, the place I had in my human's loving heart, of which there seemed no bounds….

Author Anonymous

While my experience was a tragic and sad one in the beginning, I learned so much about myself. As poet Maya Angelou has said, "I wouldn't take nothing for my journey now."

# Restoring Balance

It has taken me four years to write this book, because of all the feelings and emotions I had to process. Bella passed exactly four years ago this February.

Grief is different for everyone. Don't let anyone tell you to get over it or convince you that you've been sad too long. Some might have read this book and thought while reading it that it was a bit much to go through for a dog, but this has been my journey and it healed me on so many levels. I feel all things happen for a reason. They are to teach us, to help us grow.

Each day since Bella's passing, a new feeling or awareness has occurred. Each day I healed another part of my grief and myself a bit more. I connected with others that I might not have otherwise. I felt my feelings and did not let them get stuffed away.

Some people take years or never stop grieving for their loved ones. If you allow yourself to go deep and feel everything at the time of loss or whenever sadness arises, you can find joy again much sooner. While my deep sadness only lasted a few months, I still have sad moments from time to time when I think of things Bella would have enjoyed. I would still love for her to be a part of my life in the physical today. I am sure many feel this way.

I remember speaking to a woman the day after Bella died. She had lost her pet chihuahua and called when she heard my news, even though we didn't know each other well. She cried loudly throughout the entire conversation. She said she missed her pet so much it was as though he had just died. I asked how long had it been since he passed. She said seven years. Seven years! I believe she was holding on to something from her past that was keeping her from moving on with her life. She had not found balance.

I watched a movie called *The Changeling*, starring Angelina Jolie, a powerful movie about the loss of a child. I went in with no idea what the movie was about; I just knew that Angelina had been nominated for an Academy Award so wanted to see it. She was superb as a mother whose child was abducted. She searched for him but he was never found, so she never had any closure. Someone had seen her son alive so that gave her hope – most likely until her death. It was based on a heart-wrenching true story. It made me realize how important it was for me to see Bella when she died. If I hadn't been given that opportunity, I would still be looking for her and wondering who had her, where she might be, and if there was still something I could do to find her.

My heart goes out to those who were not able to see their loved ones before they passed, like the families of 9/11. I know it must be difficult but in some way I feel those souls did not want their families to see them that way. Remember your loved ones at their best, knowing their spirit is always with you. It never dies. They are a part of you.

Bella's passing was so significant as it demonstrated to me how much I needed a pet in my life for the often lonely times I had. An avid reader, I read this quote by Carl Jung which I thought made such sense.

> "Loneliness does not come from having no people around you but from being unable to communicate the things that seem important to you."

Share your feelings with those who care and support you. I feel ready now to restore the sense of imbalance I felt when my pet tragically died with things that make me happy like my new furry family members. I feel back to center. I look forward to the day when we will all meet again.

It took me a month after Bella's death to put a memorial book together. In it, I placed all the lovely cards people sent me, her dress, dog tags, photos of her life, and this letter:

*For My Dear Bella:*

*You brought so much joy, love, and laughter to my life. No pet will ever replace you. You are missed for your constant companionship, unconditional love, and never-ending affection. You taught me so much about being present in the moment, being spontaneous, playful, patient, affectionate, and most of all about love. I wish you joy in your new life.*

*Feel free to visit anytime. You will forever be in my heart.*

*Love,*

*Your Mom*

Whether you have just lost a pet or someone else dear to you, I hope these words have helped you in some way. It is my intention to offer some comfort and healing.

I am off to give my pets big hugs, while I look out into Universe with a big smile for Bellaluna.

May balance be restored to your life harmoniously. Sending you feng shui blessings.

## The Rainbow Bridge

There is a bridge connecting Heaven and Earth. It is called the Rainbow Bridge because of its many colors.

When a beloved pet dies, the pet goes to this place.

You have been seen, and when you and
your special friend meet, you take him
or her in your arms and embrace.

Then you cross the Rainbow Bridge
together, never again to be separated.

CPSIA information can be obtained at www.ICGtesting.com
Printed in the USA
LVOW13s2310170813

348301LV00001B/1/P